Echoes of
Eternity

A CONTEMPLATIVE JOURNAL
FOR EVERY DAY

Echoes of
Eternity

HAL M. HELMS

Quiet your heart and listen

PARACLETE PRESS
BREWSTER, MASSACHUSETTS

2016 First Printing

Echoes of Eternity: A Contemplative Journal for Every Day

Copyright © 2016 by The Community of Jesus

ISBN 978-1-61261-840-1

10 9 8 7 6 5 4 3 2 1

Published by Paraclete Press
Brewster, Massachusetts
www.paracletepress.com
Printed in the United States of America

*"Trust God from the bottom of your heart;
don't try to figure out everything on your own.
Listen for God's voice in everything you do . . ."*

Introduction

In the twenty years since the two-volume *Echoes of Eternity* was first published, thousands of people have been blessed as they read and prayed over the daily words that Hal M. Helms received and recorded for us. Those of us who knew Hal and his unassuming walk with God, first discovered the deeper reality of his spiritual life through these two books that were published just before and just after his death. For most of his life, Hal spent time daily in prayer, seeking answers from God for issues he was facing in his own life.

He wrote down answers from God in his personal journals, never with any intention of publishing them. At the request of a friend, he agreed to their publication, and the result has blessed over 50,000 readers.

One of his favorite Scripture verses was this one that stands as a wonderful invitation: . . . "[I]f you hear my voice and open the door, I will come in to you and eat with you, and you with me. . . . Let anyone who has an ear listen to what the Spirit is saying to the churches." (Revelation 3:20b, 22)

This new one-year journal takes selections from both of the original volumes—the "red" and the "blue" *Echoes* as we fondly refer to them—and offers readers the opportunity to write down what they hear God speaking to them.

We have increased the size of the book and placed only one daily selection on each page, in order to leave sufficient space for a written reflection. We have "mildly modernized" the language, as Hal did with so many Christian classics, and we have used a more contemporary version of the Bible—the *New Revised Standard Version*—for the biblical references.

Our hope is that those of you who have already found *Echoes* to be a daily companion will find this to be a fresh and engaging approach. For those who are reading *Echoes* for the first time, we hope you will find it a new, rich experience of hearing God speaking words of encouragement to you. And for all of us, may this journal be an additional incentive to listen throughout the day for what God is saying to us.

JANUARY

Morning has broken
    like the first morning,
Blackbird has spoken
    like the first bird.
Praise for the singing!
Praise for the morning!
Praise for them, springing
    fresh from the Word!

Sweet the rain's new fall
    sunlit from heaven,
Like the first dewfall
    on the first grass.
Praise for the sweetness
    of the wet garden,
Sprung in completeness
    where his feet pass.

Mine is the sunlight!
    Mine is the morning,
born of the one light
    Eden saw play!
Praise with elation,
praise every morning,
God's re-creation
    of the new day!

—Eleanor Farjeon, 1881–1965

January First

LORD, you have been our dwelling place in all generations.
—Psalm 90:1

Have no fear for tomorrow, my child. Tomorrow will hold only what I bring or allow in your life. All your tomorrows are in my hand. I am the Lord of the years. My hand is a gracious hand and all my ways are faithfulness.

As long as you keep your eyes focused on minor pains and difficulties in your path, you rob yourself of the joy of my fellowship—the communion of the Holy Spirit. You are meant to walk in a different realm—the larger reality of my kingdom. This is not an imaginary place. It is a present reality that is open to my children who seek and find it. Doubt and self-pity close off this reality from you, but they do not, cannot, destroy it. So seek and find, my child. Seek and find what hitherto you have only dimly grasped.

January Second

For surely I know the plans I have for you, says the LORD, plans for your welfare and not for harm, to give you a future with hope.
—Jeremiah 29:11

In the year that lies ahead there will be many wonders. You will see my hand unmistakably at work in your midst. Flinch not before my judgments, and do not let the enemy's accusations lodge in your heart. Be patient under my discipline, for it is for your eternal good. My goodness will not fail you and grace will always abound. Some will fall away, for they are not grounded in me. Their going may bring pain, but it will bring no loss. There must be a deeper, firmer reliance on me rather than on secondary causes. Your pride must be dealt with or it will destroy what I have given you. This is my word and I will fulfill it.

January Third

. . . but where sin increased, grace abounded all the more, so that,
just as sin exercised dominion in death, so grace might also
exercise dominion through justification leading to eternal
life through Jesus Christ our Lord.
—Romans 5:20b–21

Why are you cast down, my child, in these peaceful circumstances around you? Why do you linger over hurts and jealousies, when my peace and my joy are yours? Old sin patterns die hard—but they *do* die if that is the desire of your heart.

January Fourth

For you, O Lord, are my hope, my trust, O LORD, from my youth.
—Psalm 71:5

My child, I have not abandoned you. In your fear you felt cut off and alone. But I was there, and will be there no matter what your feelings tell you. Yes, I am speaking to you. This is not a construct of your wishful thinking.

You wonder what purpose could be served in such an experience as you had. First, you must learn to be more obedient. You give in much too easily to feelings of tiredness. Second, you must learn to bring your thoughts into captivity to my sovereign Spirit. "I will repay you for the years that the swarming locust has eaten" (Joel 2:25a)—are much, very much, involved here.

Be of good courage. All is not lost. Only pride and shallow faith—but what are they?

January Fifth

*". . . first be reconciled to your brother or sister,
and then come and offer your gift."*
—Matthew 5:24b

Put away hateful thoughts. They corrode and eat away the very foundation of your soul. Fight against the feelings of hurt and outrage, and turn every thought that would lead to hateful thoughts into prayer. You cannot hate and really pray for someone's good at the same time.

Realize, however, that it is primarily for your own sake that you are doing this. You must guard against further indulging in hateful thoughts and feelings—even repressed ones—and pray for *good* for those who hurt or oppose you. You see examples of what can happen to a soul who did not restrain feelings of hate and vengeance. Not a pretty sight, is it? Hatred is never pretty when fully unmasked. The pleasure you derive from it cannot be compared to the *joy* you will have when you put hatred away.

January Sixth

"Surely, to obey is better than sacrifice. . . ."
—I Samuel 15:22b

Listen to me instead of your own thoughts. Your thoughts are full of anxiety and fear, fantasy and unreality. My thoughts are not as yours. "Those of steadfast mind you keep in peace" (Isaiah 26:3).

I know your circumstances—and your physical needs. My arm is not shortened that it cannot save—and I am the Lord who heals you. How many times have I told you before, yet you cringe in shadows and self-pity. Your pain is but for a season—and it is never without amelioration. So do not magnify it beyond what it is. Have a good day in spite of it by listening to me instead of your thoughts. Remember, "Those who bring thanksgiving as their sacrifice honor me" (Psalm 50:23). So offer praise continually through the day.

January Seventh

If you, O LORD, should mark iniquities, Lord, who could stand? But
there is forgiveness with you, that you may be revered.
—Psalm 130:3–4

Your fear of being wrong, my child, shows that you are not living by grace, but
by works. This is not a minor fault, but a major block in our relationship
and in your spiritual growth. Go and read again Brother Lawrence's testimony*—and let your heart absorb the truth of it.

Worrying about what others may think of you, how they react to you, puts
an obstacle between you and me. No matter how pious you may appear to others,
I see your heart, and I tell you again: your fear of being wrong shows that you
are not living by grace. Your soul is filled with accusations against my goodness.
Otherwise, there would be only a desire to please me out of gratitude, not out
of fear.

* Editor's note: Br. Lawrence's *The Practice of the Presence of God* is a Christian
classic.

January Eighth

"I am the good shepherd. I know my own and my own know me. . . ."
—John 10:14

This quiet time is my gift of love to you, my child. In spite of the multitude of distractions, it still carries the stamp of my blessing. You are receiving more than you know. Healing is taking place, fallow ground is being broken up, and the holy seed of my truth is being planted. As you see the snow gently falling to the waiting ground, so my mercies descend on your waiting soul—quietly, without noise or fanfare. This is my way.

January Ninth

If we live by the Spirit, let us also be guided by the Spirit.
—Galatians 5:25

I do not rebuke you harshly, but appeal to you as a loving Father. Learn to be content with waiting when I seem to delay in speaking. Learn that in the silence much is to be gained if you let it work for you.

Do not lose your grateful heart for these moments—they are *not* ordinary. Don't let their frequency blind you to their incomparable worth to your soul.

January Tenth

"While you have the light, believe in the light,
so that you may become children of light."
—John 12:36

Listen unto me, my dear child, and listen attentively. Learn to look with the eyes of the spirit beyond the outward shell. Let your thoughts and your words aim at what lies hidden from the natural view, and do not be confused by it. I will give you the discernment you need in order to minister life. Remember that my love and care go beyond any immediate problem. Pray that you may see with me the long view—the goal to which I am leading each child of mine. Too much attention to each single incident can cloud that vision and cause unnecessary problems.

January Eleventh

If it is possible, so far as it depends on you, live peaceably with all.
—Romans 12:18

My Spirit strives within to bring your spirit into harmony with my divine purposes. Often you are like a bird trapped or held in the hand—struggling to get free—to what? You do not know.

My Spirit strives to bring you into peace. You long for peace, but you do not know how to achieve it. Only my wisdom and my way can bring you into perfect peace—and for my way to prevail, you must give up your ways.

Do not marvel that the striving between us often leaves you confused and unsatisfied. These are indications of your lack of full surrender. The dissatisfaction is the fruit of your hold-out at some level. But I am God, and my mercy does not abandon you to your false "victory." The fruit of it in your soul is meant to warn you that losing is winning, and winning is always losing.

January Twelfth

*. . . he has made known to us the mystery of his will . . . to gather up all
things in him, things in heaven and things on earth.*
—Ephesians 1:9–10

My word brings joy even when it causes you pain. It brings life, even when
it brings death to your wonted ways. Rather, it brings joy *because* it brings
pain, and life *because* it brings death.

The deepest things of life remain a mystery to you, my child, and it must
be so. In the mystery there are realities as yet only faintly grasped or dimly
seen. But their presence assures you that there is more to life with me than
you have yet experienced.

Do not be afraid of the mysteries, and do not try to explain them away.
This foolish effort on your part has robbed you of blessings and stunted your
growth in me for many years. Expand the capacity of your soul to admit
what you cannot understand or reason out—and let my word bring the life
and joy you so much want and need.

God's word brings joy because
it brings pain, and life because
it brings death.

Admit what you cannot understand
or reason out — and let my word
bring the life and joy you so
much want and need.

January Thirteenth

O you who answer prayer! To you all flesh shall come.
—Psalm 65:2

I hear your prayer, and it shall be done. No prayer is prayed in vain. Leave the particulars to me, my child, and in my time and way your desire will be fulfilled. I am still training you in the path of faith. I still look for trust rather than doubt or questioning. A loving relationship must be built on trust—and you have ample ground for that, do you not? So keep on praying and *learning* that trust is a choice that you can make. Don't let doubts discourage you. Let my strength encourage your fearful heart.

January Fourteenth

If we live by the Spirit, let us also be guided by the Spirit.
—Galatians 5:25

I am caring for you, my child, I am caring for you. Remember, with me there are no accidents, no surprises. What comes to you unexpectedly and unbidden has been long known and foreseen by me. It comes by my permission and carries the seed of my blessing.

I bid you now to look up. Trust me beyond your understanding and knowledge. Put your hand in my fatherly hand—to be guided into what lies ahead for you. Fear not and be not troubled. I am faithful, and will not leave or forsake you.

January Fifteenth

Do you not realize that God's kindness is meant
to lead you to repentance?
—Romans 2:4b

Vain regret is not repentance. Yes, you have made many wrong choices through the course of your life. But I have no pleasure in the self-pity of remorse. Since my grace has never been lacking and my mercy has never been withdrawn from you, your life has been a redeemed life. It does not mean that the wrong choices brought no harm—they did and do. But my grace has been and is greater, and those choices did not overrule it.

My gift of repentance, unlike vain regret, is a forward-looking attitude. It enables you to lay hold of my future, cleansed and freed from paralyzing guilt and shame. Claim it, my child, and let your tears be tears of joy and gratitude.

January Sixteenth

Rejoice in the Lord always; again I will say, Rejoice.
—Philippians 4:4

Praise is the best medicine, but praise must be from the right motive. It must not be thought of as a source of blessing and healing, even though they are its by-products. Praise must come from your gratitude for my many mercies, and for specific ones. Let it well up from your heart and unite with the universal song from all the ages past—an eternal alleluia. Let it drown out the little voices of woe and complaint that run around in your head. Let praise draw you out of concern with your physical condition—and thus be a foretaste of my victory over them all. Praise is work for you, my child, because you have done so little of it in your life. Redeem the time you have left on earth—let your mouth and your heart be filled with my praise.

January Seventeenth

*Blessed be the God and Father of our Lord Jesus Christ,
the Father of mercies and the God of all consolation,
who consoles us in all our affliction. . . .*
—2 Corinthians 1:3–4a

Bring them to me, my child, bring them to me—the wounds of the past, the painful memories of foolish choices, the hurtful wrongs you inflicted on others—all that burdens your soul with sad regrets. It was for sinners that I came to this earth. It was for the undone, the heavy-laden souls who knew no relief from the pain of their wrongness.

The crucifixion you feel as these old memories return is a crucifixion of pride. The humiliation and shame are but necessary blows to the nature that still seeks to be "somebody." As you bury the memories in my wounds, there is no place for boasting or vainglory. Neither is there any reason to continue to nurture the pain. Gratitude, praise, and expectation can replace the defeating deadness of old regrets.

January Eighteenth

"For everyone who asks receives. . . ."
—Matthew 7:8a

Ask and it will be given you. Be bolder in your asking, my child, for I take pleasure in granting the requests of my children. Asking is a way of expressing your faith in me and in my goodwill toward you. Take your eyes off the "impossibilities" of circumstances, and ask for what I put in your heart to ask. The process is vital to your maturing and deepening in faith.

Make a record of the big and small things you pray for, so that you will know the surety of what I am saying to you. Ask and believe!

January Nineteenth

*Let us therefore approach the throne of grace with boldness, so that we
may receive mercy and find grace to help in time of need.*
—Hebrews 4:16

My dear child, you are troubled about many things—and about one thing:
your fear of what lies ahead for you and your ability to cope with it. You
do not have to cope alone—as you have seen in weeks past. I bid you be of
good cheer. Let the promises work for you. Do not negate them by refusing
to believe. Remember Israel in the wilderness. They did not enter into the
Promised Land because of their unbelief. You do not need to make the same
bad choice!

January Twentieth

Trust in the LORD, and do good; so you will live in the land,
and enjoy security. Take delight in the LORD, and he will
give you the desires of your heart.
—Psalm 37:3–4

My light is shining on your way. My path is unfolding before you as you walk with me. You do not need to see ahead, and it would be harmful to you if you could. My way and my wisdom are always best. Do not fear what lies on the path. The darkness will disappear at the right time, and you will see everything you need to see. No harm can come to the soul that is in my care. No harm can come to you as long as you stay with me.

January Twenty-first

See, I have inscribed you on the palms of my hands;
your walls are continually before me.
—Isaiah 49:16

My child, I have told you, you are inscribed on my hand—my right hand. By this I mean to subdue every fear and doubt you have about your life in me. "Whoever fears has not reached perfection in love" (1 John 4:18b). That is a message to you in the first place, so that you bear in mind the inner work you must still do. Love is active, not passive—and you have become much, much too passive. Exercise your love—such as it is—so that it might fill a greater space in you. Stop quenching the Spirit and act on the intuitive thoughts that come to you. In loving your neighbor as yourself, you will drive out the arrogant self-concern that characterizes your life. Since I remember you, you can afford to forget you. Make a stab at it today!

January Twenty-second

. . . for he does not willingly afflict or grieve anyone.
—Lamentations 3:33

I tell you truly, I share the sorrow of your heart for those you love who walk in the darkness of this world. The pain you feel is only a minor portion of mine, and there is no way to avoid the suffering. I know my plans for them, which you do not, but you can trust my infinite mercy and wisdom to act. In the meantime, without being frivolous and irresponsible, you can keep lifting them up to me. Remember that "the prayer of the righteous is powerful and effective" (James 5:16b).

All this will work together for good for you and for those for whom you are praying, and my glory will be seen. Nothing worthwhile comes without struggle and pain since sin entered my world. But in spite of it all, I still love my creation and my plans for it are good.

My dear child, rest in me.

Lift up: Dick, John & Gloria, Erin, Josh & Keegan + baby girl, Katie & Andy

January Twenty-third

. . . let us lay also aside every weight and the sin that clings so closely,
and let us run with patience the race that is set before us. . . .
—Hebrews 12:1b

The riches of my kingdom are for the poor. They are hidden from those who come laden with their own gifts. That is why, my child, you are required to wait while we strip from you the weight of your internal wealth. Each time you are required to wait for my inner voice, you become aware anew of your own poverty of spirit. You face the deadness of your soul apart from my quickening power—and the suffering opens you to be blessed by my refreshing grace.

O you of little faith! When will you learn to take each moment as it comes without faltering or whining at what it might turn out to be? Your lack of trust is a great handicap, and it is organically tied with your "inner wealth" that turns out to be dust and ashes. The riches of my kingdom are for the poor.

January Twenty-fourth

. . . no evil shall befall you, no scourge come near your tent.
—Psalm 91:10

"No evil shall befall you, no scourge come near your tent." The prayers of others have often shielded you, though you knew nothing about it. The faithfulness of others has formed an easier path for you to follow. Be faithful, then, my child, in your watch. Hold up those for whom I have given you responsibility. Link your prayers with the faithful around and before you—that my will may be accomplished "on earth as it is in heaven" (Matthew 6:10b).

You still have much to learn about the mystery and marvel and might of prayer. These things are hidden from the wise, but are made known to "babes and infants" (Psalm 8:2)—to those who are small in their own eyes and are teachable.

January Twenty-fifth

But nothing unclean will enter it, nor anyone who practices abomination
or falsehood, but only those who are written in the Lamb's book of life.
—Revelation 21:27

As the sun shines on the earth, bringing light and unveiling the darkness,
so does my Spirit shine upon your soul. Dark recesses are hidden from your
consciousness, but they are not hidden from me. The cleansing, purifying
work of light must go on to prepare you for your eternal home. "But nothing unclean will enter it." So the cleansing is an important part of your
preparation.

Do not fear this process, my child. Already you know that each step
brings release and greater freedom within. There are still ties that keep you
from a full realization of my perfect work, but do not despair nor grow discouraged. That would only slow down the process. Be honest with yourself
and seek the Spirit of Truth in facing all accusations. He convicts, cleanses,
and sets free.

January Twenty-sixth

The light shines in the darkness, and the
darkness did not overcome it.
—John 1:5

The day has dawned with the light of my love. Darkness cannot hold it back because I am its light. Your fears about the future are futile, for the future is in my hand. Every time you give way to foreboding, you abandon the faith ground I have provided for you.

My dear child, can you stop loving your children? Neither can I stop loving mine. It is my nature to love, and so I counsel you again: leave the future to me—your future and your loved ones' future. I care, and will care. Be at peace.

Go forward into the day without fear. I go before you and prepare your way. There are no surprises for me in the events of the day, even though they may surprise or even startle you. Keep your perspective. Do not allow the enemy to gain a stronghold through your imagination. Let the truth be your *shield and buckler* (Psalm 91:4). Remember, my child, you are mine and the day is mine.

January Twenty-seventh

Avoid the profane chatter and contradictions of
what is falsely called knowledge. . . .
—I Timothy 6:20b

My word is often turned aside because it appears too simple. I come to you in simplicity in order to cut across the false reasoning you have allowed to grow up over many years. You come to me and complain of feeling dead and empty. Yet the truth is, you are full of many things—mainly yourself. Emptying out results in your feeling less empty.

Keep it simple today, my child. Do not yield to the temptation to try to appear profound. I know the way you should walk, so let me guide and lead.

January Twenty-eighth

For in hope we were saved.
—Romans 8:24a

Do not cast away your hope, my child, for I am its source and its fulfillment. It is I who put hope in your heart, and those who hold fast their hope shall not be confounded. The fractured image of reality you now see will one day be replaced by a clear, undistorted vision. You cannot see the whole picture, but what you see is enough.

January Twenty-ninth

*Although he causes grief, he will have compassion
according to the abundance of his steadfast love. . . .*
—Lamentations 3:32

In the shadow of my hand, pain. In the touch of my hand, healing. Sometimes the shadow lingers and pain is prolonged. Will you trust me in the shadow as well as in the sun? Can you walk with me over rough ways and not complain? Comfort is a fleeting thing. Struggle brings inner strength. I do not want you to be consumed with attention on the difficulties of your life. They are yet minor in comparison with what many are called to endure. Rather choose to believe that shadows pass. My good will prevails, and your feeble faith is not in vain.

January Thirtieth

I have loved you with an everlasting love; therefore
I have continued my faithfulness to you.
—Jeremiah 31:3b

My children, my children, I love you. My joy in you is not complete until you know and comprehend that love. It is a love that passes knowledge, and I invite you all to journey past mere knowledge into that fullness of love. Do not be afraid of love, my children. Be afraid rather of your closed, protective shells that shut out my sun. Do not be afraid of being kind to one another, of making allowances for weaknesses and wounds not yet fully healed. Beware of self-righteousness, for it bears bitter fruit. Sing and rejoice in the Love that sought and found you. It will not lead you astray.

January Thirty-first

Before I was humbled I went astray, but now I keep your word.
—Psalm 119:67

My child, do not despise my corrections. They are sent for your ultimate good, painful and difficult as they are for you. I have not forgotten to be gracious, and I am not absent from any trial you are being asked to endure. As Abraham found, my eye is upon you, and when the work is done, my answer is there, waiting to be revealed.

"The secret of the Lord is with them that fear him" (Psalm 25:14 KJV). This holy fear is a protection against that part of your nature that would carry you into complete darkness. Cherish it, and tremble before my Word. Cherish it, and let it be a protection to you, like a wall around a sheltered garden. You will come to know and trust me more and more if you will not despise my corrections.

FEBRUARY

I come to the garden alone,
    While the dew is still on the roses;
And the voice I hear, ringing on my ear,
    The Son of God discloses;

He speaks and the sound of his voice
    Is so sweet the birds hush their singing,
And the melody that he gave to me,
    Within my heart is ringing.

I'd stay in the garden with him
    Though the night around me be falling,
But he bids me go; through the voice of woe,
    His voice to me is calling.

And he walks with me, and he talks with me,
    And he tells me I am His own.
And the joy we share as we tarry there,
    None other has ever known.

—C. Austin Miles, 1868–1946

February First

O come, let us worship and bow down, let us kneel
before the LORD, our Maker.
—Psalm 95:6

The bowed head and contrite heart are fitting as you wait for my word. They are fitting, too, before the circumstances I will to place in your path. Your head does not bow easily—for you still long to be in charge. Little do you realize the hold that desire has on your life, and the peace you forfeit as a result. Esau despised his birthright for a mess of pottage. You forfeit yours for less!! O my dear child, learn to bow the head. Learn to bow the heart! My way truly is best.

February Second

They rise in the darkness as a light for the upright;
they are gracious, merciful, and righteous.
—Psalm 112:4

Light arises in the darkness for those who love me. No threat can thwart the ongoing fulfillment of my will. Say to those of a fearful heart: Behold your King! Have I failed you in the past? Has my help been withheld from your cry? Let everything conspire to propel you forward in the path I have laid out for you. No, you cannot see the distant end—but there is light on your path today. Keep your eye on the light, and the darkness will lose its power to trouble you.

February Third

*"And when he [the Comforter] comes, he will prove the world wrong
about sin and righteousness and judgment. . . ."*
—John 16:8

I come not to praise you nor to condemn you, but to build you up in spirit.
Your adversary would use both praise and condemnation to confound you
and tear you down. The memory of past sins should not linger, but hasten
you to thankfulness for forgiveness and mercy. The sobering reminders of
your wrong choices should keep you from being proud. Remembering who
you are is not a cause for despair, but for wonder. My presence in your life
has saved you from many disasters—so let them remind you that your help
has been, is, and ever shall be from me.

February Fourth

"You of little faith, why did you doubt?"
—Matthew 14:31b

Never doubt my goodness. That is one of the chief ploys of your adversary—to insert questions in your mind about me. He knows where to attack at the weak places in your spiritual armor—which are the "strong" places in yourself. What folly to allow his little game to triumph over you, when you have a Strong Deliverer! O my child, I wish that you would settle it once for all—that my goodness never fails. I am who I am, and I change not. Never, *never* doubt my goodness!

February Fifth

"All mine are yours, and yours are mine;
and I have been glorified in them."
—John 17:10

All are mine—the living and the dead. Those who have gone from your sight and left their bodies to return to dust still live in my sight. You are connected with the unseen world with ties that were made during their earthly life span. You are never alone in that sense, my child.

You have tended to think of your life as a solo performance. That is a grave misunderstanding. Whenever you can, you should strengthen the inner sense of connectedness with your companions. Loneliness is not inevitable. Once you catch the vision of being part of the great company, not imaginary or mystical, but *real*, you will begin to experience the benefits I planned in my divine scheme of things. Don't be afraid of "the company of heaven," my child. It is *real*, and you are called to be part of it one day.

February Sixth

O give thanks to the LORD, for he is good;
for his steadfast love endures forever.
—I Chronicles 16:34

Thanks and praise suit the upright. Thanks and praise suit the sinner. Forgiveness produces a thankful heart. Never cease to lift your heart in grateful remembrance of what I have done for you, my child, for this is your safeguard. Once the well of thankfulness goes dry or is clogged through misuse, disobedience is not far behind, and with it, all the sorrows and pain it entails; you need to practice praise. Your identity and welfare are intimately tied up in it. Praise is not a luxury. It is as vital as the air.

February Seventh

"Go; let it be done for you according to your faith."
—Matthew 8:13b

Believing and receiving go hand in hand, my child. Just as the radio must be tuned to a certain frequency to pick up a particular station, so, in a manner of speaking, your heart must be *attuned* to me. Believing opens up your receiving capacity. Without it, you are shut off and have only your own thoughts and reasonings. Because you have set such great confidence in reasoning and being reasonable, belief does not come easily for you. You must "go against the grain" of years to achieve the blessed state of being "as a little child." But that, my child, is where believing and receiving can meet—to your good and my glory.

February Eighth

*Let us therefore approach the throne of grace with boldness, so that we
may receive mercy and find grace to help in time of need.*
—Hebrews 4:16

My dear child, know that I love you. You long to be loved, and yet you are afraid
of love, and close your heart against me and those who seek admission. You *need*
my love, not just as an objective reality—which it is—but as a subjective, inner
heart experience, which you do not, for the most part, have. I say this not to
condemn you, but to invite you to open the door that I may comfort and sustain
you in your times of need.

February Ninth

*Trust in the LORD forever, for in the LORD GOD you
have an everlasting rock.*
—Isaiah 26:4

As you move through the day, be aware of me. Listen in your heart for that "still, small voice." Let me check your impulsive and cruel reactions to others. Become aware that you *are* hurtful and hateful when your pride is hurt. Let me be your inner Companion and Guard against this side of you. I have only plans for good, so do not expect evil from me—you do not need to defend yourself or your ideas.

February Tenth

Deep calls to deep at the thunder of your cataracts; all your
waves and your billows have gone over me.
—Psalm 42:7

Heart to heart, and Spirit to spirit, our fellowship does not always need words. When you are at peace in my presence, know that I am communing with you. And when words fail you in prayer, remember that the Spirit searches the heart and prays with groanings that are to you, wordless. I am ever ready to hear the cry of need and the voice of genuine praise.

February Eleventh

This is the day that the LORD has made; let us rejoice and be glad in it.
—Psalm 118:24

Truly I tell you, you are mine. I bought you with a great price: my own blood. You find it embarrassing to hear such tender words. This is what I meant when I told you that love means letting in. It is not your worthiness that is the issue. It is not to set you up in the wrong way. It is to heal the inner wounds and fill the inner emptiness that I speak to you in this way. Open your heart to me, my child, and let us become acquainted with one another.

February Twelfth

*Then Jesus told them a parable about their need to
pray always and not to lose heart.*
—Luke 18:1

My dear child, I raise dead souls to new life. Your own feeling of deadness
is a necessary preparation to help you receive and recognize my coming.

You wonder why you have not made more progress in your prayer life. It is
because you do not yet want this more than you want other things. You still have
a desire for power—power to change things according to your understanding. For
your own sake, my child, I have not allowed this. Say "No" to it, painful as it feels.
Learn from others how they have given it up. Come with me into the place of yield-
edness—for only there will you enjoy the vital life my presence brings.

February Thirteenth

For God alone my soul waits in silence, for my hope is from him.
—Psalm 62:5

Expect a blessing—that is the faith attitude I am pleased with when you come to pray. You would not go repeatedly to someone with a request you did not expect to be received favorably. Likewise, my child, when you approach the throne of grace, I want that expectancy to flood your heart. With such sacrifice I am well pleased. The sacrifice involved is the laying down of your old fear-filled, guilt-laden thoughts. I have promised that those who *trust* in me will not be confounded. So come to me *expecting* me to fulfill my word.

February Fourteenth

We know that the whole creation has been groaning
in labor pains until now. . . .
—Romans 8:22

Yes, my child, the world is full of pain and suffering. Do not think that I have forgotten it, or that my heart is unmoved by the cries of my children. It is not for you to understand my ways and my delays. It is for you to keep on looking to me for your daily needs, and to be faithful in holding up the bundle of concerns I have laid on your heart.

One day your eyes will be opened to see what is now hidden from your view. In the meantime, do not turn your heart away from the suffering you see in this world. Turn every sight of pain and hurt into prayer. Learn to transform the pain into petition, knowing that I am at work to bring good out of every evil.

February Fifteenth

For my thoughts are not your thoughts, nor are your
ways my ways, says the LORD.
—Isaiah 55:8

Yes, my child, my mercies are beyond numbering and they are new every morning. It is my pleasure to do good things to my children and for my children. Just as you desire good for yours, I seek the good for mine. For my ways are not your ways—and thereby you often become confused. You think of me as one like yourself—but my love is a pure love—not contaminated with self and sin and guilt as yours is. So, as my love and my ever-new mercies operate in your life and in the life of your loved ones, learn to entrust them *and* yourself to my tender care. Only then can you know the "peace of God, which surpasses all understanding" (Philippians 4:7a)—for your peace will not depend on your understanding.

February Sixteenth

Search me, O God, and know my heart; test me and know
my thoughts. See if there is any wicked way in me. . . .
—Psalm 139:23–24a

I am your Sun, your everlasting Light. When your heart is turned toward me, my light illumines your soul. There you see many faults, many wounds, much that is not beautiful. This must be, my child, because the work is not yet complete. You cannot expose yourself to my light without this consequence. Your prayer, "See if there is any wicked way in me" (Psalm 139:24a), is fulfilled each time you allow my light to shine in your heart.

Just as the sunlight destroys that which lives in darkness on this earth, the sunlight of my presence does its work in your soul. And so, though there is still much to do, and the faults and wounds are many, the healing and cleansing are going on and will go on as you turn your heart to my light.

February Seventeenth

*. . . in order to make [the church] holy by cleansing her with
the washing of water by the word. . . .*
—Ephesians 5:26

The cleansing of the soul is a long process. The stain of sin goes very deep, and surface cleansing is only part of the process. You get discouraged that old sinful thoughts and temptations keep coming back. You are to learn to fight their early appearance more aggressively. Bring them to me, my child, for you cannot handle them alone. Confess—do not deny nor repress—but confess them and place them under my cleansing blood. "Sinners washed beneath this flood lose all their guilty stains" (William Cowper). This is an ongoing work of my grace, and I expect your full participation if you want to be prepared for the light I have in store for you and for "all who have longed for [my] appearing" (2 Timothy 4:8b).

February Eighteenth

My child, I do love you. Your fears and worries are needless luggage that you carry on your trip through life. I would that you let me take them from you, that your freedom might be a testimony to others. Bring your fears and worries to me, my child, and let me deal with them. They are too much for you.

February Nineteenth

Let us therefore approach the throne of grace with boldness, so that we may receive mercy and find grace to help in time of need.
—Hebrews 4:16

My dear child, whenever you come to me in prayer, whatever condition your soul may be in, come boldly and with full confidence. Drawing back, for whatever reason, is a form of rejection of me and my love. False humility has no place in this relationship. I know you better than you know yourself. If I had put our relationship on the basis of your deserving, it would never have begun. So, in the words of my Word, "approach the throne of grace with boldness, so that [you] may receive mercy and find grace to help in time of need."

February Twentieth

There is no fear in love, but perfect love casts out fear. . . .
—I John 4:18a

This is my word for today: just as love casts out fear, fear casts out love. You cannot love when fear is in control. You are not fighting your fear-filled thoughts hard enough. You too readily give ground to them. I bid you to remember—remember where you have been and what I have brought you through. Remember and rejoice—even when you can't see how things are going to work out in the present.

February Twenty-first

"According to your faith let it be done to you."
—Matthew 9:29b

Your trouble in receiving, my child, is your trouble in believing. Not only these words that I give you day by day, but many other gifts I would freely give in answer to childlike faith. "The simple heart that freely asks in love, receives" (John G. Whittier).

I seek a people who are not afraid to believe boldly. History is a record of my faithful response to this kind of bold praying. I see instead the tendency to rely on human schemes and worldly wisdom—and there is no simple, bold faith in that. So my blessing is delayed or its magnitude is diminished. "According to your faith let it be done to you."

I set "impossible" goals before you to prove my power and goodness. You say, "They shall celebrate the fame of your abundant goodness" (Psalm 145:7a). Why? Because they were faced with their own limits and my limitless goodness. Think on these things today, my child, and grow more simple.

February Twenty-second

"[T]here is need of only one thing. Mary has chosen the better part,
which will not be taken away from her."
—Luke 10:42

My child, you have chosen the better part. I say this to encourage you, not to puff you up in your own mind. You and I know who and what you are in yourself. But my grace has prevailed to give you a holy desire not to let your nature prevail. The better part requires a discipline you have yet to master. It requires a steadiness you have not yet achieved. Yes, *achieved*, for it is my plan and my gracious provision to allow you to achieve and be blessed through it. This is why passivity before the many assaults to your soul is so wrong. It is an ungodly surrender, an unnecessary one. I will show you how to fight, and will prompt you when the enemy comes—only be ready to follow through with me in the battle.

February Twenty-third

*. . . we look not at what can be seen but at what cannot
be seen; for what can be seen is temporary, but
what cannot be seen is eternal.*
—2 Corinthians 4:18

Turn your eyes away from the drabness of the day and look at the brightness of my dwelling. I dwell in the high and holy place—and that means that where I am there is all the brightness and beauty you could desire. And I dwell with those who are of lowly and contrite hearts (Isaiah 57:15)—which means that my beauty and glory will be yours to the extent that you have a contrite heart.

February Twenty-fourth

"The eye is the lamp of the body. So, if your eye is healthy, your whole body will be full of light. . . ."
—Matthew 6:22

The eye is a precious gift. It allows the many wonders and beauty of the created world to enter your mind and soul. You are spiritually affected by what the eye sees. And herein lies the problem. Your mind is not disciplined to focus on the inner vision. It grabs what the eye conducts to it and runs in many directions, always ending in *self.* This makes it a serious distraction, and is one of the reasons for praying with closed eyes. Even this is not a sure shield against distraction, for your mind will still process images stored in its memory.

Do not despair, my child, but do not accept this condition as unchangeable. Keep working at getting the inner vision calm, stable, and stayed on me. It will not be easy, but nothing worthwhile comes without struggle.

February Twenty-fifth

Thus says the LORD: In a time of favor I have answered you,
on a day of salvation I have helped you. . . .
—Isaiah 49:8a

None ever called on me in vain. None. Though they did not know me, though they may never have realized that their cry was heard, their call was not in vain. My ears are open to the cries of all my children, and my heart is open to their needs. Do not think that I am unmoved at the sight of the suffering in the world.

Today I give you this word: trust me in all things. Everything is in my hands, and you can leave to me whatever is disturbing or troublesome to you. Trust me and seek to live in my peace.

February Twenty-sixth

For this slight momentary affliction is preparing us for an
eternal weight of glory beyond all measure....
—2 Corinthians 4:17

My mercy never runs out. It is an outflowing of my nature. I remind you of
it often because your nature imposes a false idea of me upon your heart. I
am the Good Shepherd, and I seek only the good and welfare of my flock.
Believe this, my child, and relax in my goodness. Fear brings torment and
love casts away both.

February Twenty-seventh

"For truly I tell you, if you have faith the size of a mustard seed, you will say to this mountain, 'Move from here to there,' and it will move; and nothing will be impossible for you."
—Matthew 17:20b

Oceans and mountains are no problem for me. It is harder to work a change in the human heart. Not only does sin cling closely to the heart—the heart clings closely to its sin. You experience the same old aches and longings, my child, and are lazy in your struggle to be free of them. You must struggle, because I will not violate your will and do it for you. I *will* give you the grace and strength you need, and I want you to be free of these old longings. It can take place—if you will let go.

February Twenty-eighth

All things came into being through him, and without
him not one thing came into being.
—John 1:3a

The past is past, and I have covered it with the cloak of my mercy. Vain regrets and remembered failures can only lead to a dead end if you do not accept my all-encompassing forgiveness. It is pride that keeps the pain alive in remembering how you failed people and left hurt in your wake. Rather, watch the present where the same patterns are alive in you, and be diligent in avoiding the same sins under a different guise.

February Twenty–ninth

*Although the doors were shut, Jesus came and stood among them and
said, "Peace be with you."*
—John 20:26b

I do grant you my peace, my child, as I have promised. My peace is often
hidden in the inner depths, under the turmoil of your thoughts and
fears. To find my peace, you must choose to go behind and beneath those
troublesome waves. Your human reasoning tells you such an abandonment
of "reality" is foolish if not impossible. But I tell you that it is neither
foolish nor impossible—and that true peace can only be found here. In the
world you will have tribulation—the "surface" will often be turbulent. Sink
beneath and discover.

MARCH

I heard the voice of Jesus say,
    "Come unto me and rest;
Lay down, thou weary one, lay down
    Thy head upon my breast."
I came to Jesus as I was,
    Weary and worn and sad,
I found in him a resting-place
    And he has made me glad.

I heard the voice of Jesus say,
    "Behold, I freely give
The living water, thirsty soul,
    Stoop down and drink and live."
I came to Jesus and I drank
    Of that life-giving stream;
My thirst was quenched, my soul revived,
    And now I live in him.

I heard the voice of Jesus say,
    "I am this dark world's Light;
Look unto me, thy morn shall rise,
    And all thy day be bright."
I looked to Jesus and I found
    In him my Star, my Sun;
And in that light of life I'll walk,
    Till traveling days are done.

—Horatius Bonar, 1808–1889

March First

Guard me as the apple of the eye; hide me under the
shadow of your wings. . . .
—Psalm 17:8

My child, my child, why do you doubt my love? It grieves my heart for you to question the ways of my providence. Have I not been with you in every dark place? Has there ever been an end to my amazing grace? Trust then; the future is all in my hands. The wind and the waves still obey my commands. Nothing shall touch you but by my permission. Relax and be still: that is my commission.

March Second

. . . for the fruit of the light is found in all that is
good and right and true.
—Ephesians 5:9

Stand in truth. Seek the truth and pursue it. Flee from fantasies and false-hoods, the icing on the cake of deceit. Truth often cuts, sometimes wounds, but only to heal. Do not fear the truth. Stand in it boldly. Speak it coura-geously, even when it threatens a false peace. Know that I, the Lord, am the God of truth. Know that I, the Son of God, am the truth embodied in a human life. Respect the truth—reverence and honor it—for the truth brings life.

March Third

Have mercy, my child, on those who have offended you. Remember how many times you have offended me. My way is not the grudge-bearing way, but the forgiving way. I have called you in righteousness to walk a holy way—a way that leads to life abundant, full and free. That is the prize I call you to seek. Seek it with all your heart and pay any price it may demand. Do not hate the instruments I choose to crucify your pride. Pride is the enemy—not the person who has offended you.

March Fourth

You will do well to be attentive to this as to a lamp shining in a dark place, until the day dawns and the morning star rises in your hearts.
—2 Peter 1:19b

I move through the thickets of your thoughts as a ray of light and truth for your soul. Your thoughts weave a thicket of darkness—twisted, tangled, leading nowhere. My light and my truth lead you outward and onward. Do not drag the thicket with you. I will help you cut loose from the old patterns of desire and ambition. Believe me, my child, it *can* happen if you are willing. But you must seek and desire to change. Look for the light shining through the thicket and follow where it leads.

March Fifth

Is my hand shortened, that it cannot redeem?
Or have I no power to deliver?
—Isaiah 50:2b

In the beauty of the morning my light dispels the shadows of night. In the same way my Spirit, the light of the world, dispels the shadows of your inner darkness. Where I dwell, there is light.

Your doors are doors into that darkness. Your questions are latches that open the doors into the gloom. Questions that cannot and will not be answered in this life lead to doubt and even to despair. But you can choose to set them aside and remain in the light of faith and trust. You can *choose* to walk by faith instead of insisting on walking by reason and answers to unanswerable questions. It is a humbler road, but one on which I journey with those who choose it. Be one of them, my child.

March Sixth

*"In the same way, every good tree bears good fruit, but the bad tree bears
bad fruit. Thus you will know them by their fruits."*
—Matthew 7:17, 20

The tree does not know how the fruit is made or what its end will be. Its
task is to *be* and to send its roots deep into the soil. So with you, my child.
It is not your care to be concerned about what will become of the "fruit" of
your life. Keep sending the roots into the fertile soil of my Word, and into
the living water of my Spirit. The fruit will be good, and it will bless others.
That is all you need to know—or can afford to know.

March Seventh

Praise the LORD! Praise the LORD, O my soul! I will praise the LORD
as long as I live; I will sing praises to my God all my life long.
—Psalm 146:1–2

It is my will to speak to you in your inner ear. Open, my child, to my voice.
You do not make it happen, but you *can* prevent it, by filling your mind with
vain thoughts.

The path before you is a good path. The shadows in the valley through
which you have come are meant to urge you to seek the light—the light of
my truth and my mercy. Do not carry the shadows with you as you emerge
into this next chapter of your life. My sunlight radiates and drives out the
doubts and fears. *Let, allow, permit* my goodness to dominate your soul. Work
at it, my child, for your sake and for the fulfilling of my will through you.

March Eighth

So if anyone is in Christ, there is a new creation: everything old has passed away; see, everything has become new!
—2 Corinthians 5:17

Eternal peace is found in my presence. Here you will find rest from turmoil and a cure for the restlessness of your heart. Seek this peace more frequently, my child, for in it lies my healing, my wisdom, and my strength.

March Ninth

My soul melts away for sorrow; strengthen me according to your word.
—Psalm 119:28

I will strengthen you, I will help you, I will uphold you with my victorious right hand (Isaiah 41:10). That is my word to you today.

March Tenth

"My grace is sufficient for you, for power is made perfect in weakness."
—2 Corinthians 12:9b

I am here. I have come according to my promised answer to your prayer. I am acquainted with all your ways and your thoughts—the desires and longings of your heart. I am the Merciful One and do not despise your feeble prayers.

Continue to look expectantly rather than fearfully to the future. On the one hand you maintain a positive and hopeful outlook, but you also carry dark forebodings and groundless fears.

Remember, my child, it is the prayer of *faith* that moves mountains.

Enter into this mystery more fully, and prove me, that I am able to do more abundantly than you ask or think.

March Eleventh

For in him all the fullness of God was pleased to dwell, and through him God was pleased to reconcile to himself all things, whether on earth or in heaven, by making peace through the blood of the cross.
—Colossians 1:19–20

In this sign you will conquer (Constantine). In my cross is your victory. Mine is a finished work. Mine is a perfect work. And it is yours, my child, as my gift of love to you. There is no other victory. There is only striving after emptiness and wind. Blessed are you if you know this victory and remain faithful to it.

Do not chafe at the restrictions my cross lays upon you. Yield quickly to my way and let not your heart be troubled. I see all and know all—and I am with you every step of your way. *In this sign you will conquer.*

March Twelfth

"Then the son said to him, 'Father, I have sinned against heaven and before you; I am no longer worthy to be called your son.' But the father said, . . . '[l]et us eat and celebrate; for this son of mine was dead and is alive again; he was lost, and is found.'"
—Luke 15:21–24a

Listening is hard for you, because you have always had many thoughts of your own—or so you supposed, not knowing how to discern those that came from me. Each day you come to me with much doubt and inner restraint. It is as though you come with your ears stuffed with cotton, and only slowly take it away that you might begin to hear me. I have told you that I am not reluctant to speak to you. It is your reluctance to hear that causes the long delay. Notice that when the cotton is out, my words come through without delay.

My child, you are still in doubt of my love and care for you. You are still in the "slave" position—acting in fear and hiding. I invite you home, my child. You have always craved a home—and I tell you truly, your true home is with me. Nothing else will satisfy that inner yearning. Come home, and quickly begin to accept my divine, fatherly care. Live as a beloved child and not as a slave!

March Thirteenth

*. . . just as he chose us in Christ before the foundation of the world
to be holy and blameless before him in love.*
—Ephesians 1:4

In the course of your life, my hand has overshadowed you and protected you. My tender mercies have attended you and spared you. Do not ask why, or doubt that it is so. As you review the past, make it a sure foundation with which to face the future. The foundation is my overarching, unfailing love and care—a foundation that cannot fail.

March Fourteenth

[God said,] "Therefore come out from them, and be separate from them, says the Lord, and touch nothing unclean; then I will welcome you, and I will be your father, and you shall be my sons and daughters, says the Lord Almighty."
—2 Corinthians 6:17–18

I have heard your prayer and your desire for more conscious dialog between us. You hold the key to this—and if you are willing to follow me, it shall be so.

Do not marvel that I, the Lord of heaven and earth, leave this matter in your hands and heart. It is an expression of the dignity I have bestowed on my created sons and daughters. I have yielded to your key decisions in our relationship, so that the relationship may be based on grace and free choice. Only choices freely made can open the door to the goal I have in mind for you.

Another thing: do not worry so much about getting things all right. Of course you will make mistakes. You are hard of hearing, aren't you? But my love for you is great enough to protect you from serious errors or misinterpretation. Children stumble and fall as they learn to walk, and after all, my child, you aren't writing the Bible!

March Fifteenth

But the steadfast love of the LORD is from everlasting to everlasting on those who fear him. . . .
—Psalm 103:17a

I am the Lord who heals you. The adversary meant evil for you, but I mean everything for your good and for life. Put aside the distractions that pull you from my chosen path. Take each day as a gift of love from the giver of love. Purify your mind and thoughts with simple cries and prayers. Prove me by the waters of Meribah (Numbers 20:13). Let me turn the bitter into sweet and trust that I can ever do so. No one knows this save those who choose to become little children before their heavenly Father. The oil of my mercy never runs out.

Numbers 20:13 — These were the waters of Meribah, where the Israelites quarrel with the Lord and where he showed himself holy among them.

2017

March Sixteenth

"Lord, I am not worthy to have you come under my roof; but only
speak the word, and my servant will be healed."
—Matthew 8:8b

This is a time of healing. It is a time for the repairing of breaches. Some of them
have already begun to be repaired. Wholeness waits for my restoring grace. Do
not marvel that it is so, for I the Lord have promised and I fulfill my word. Be
keenly aware of my leadings, for you will find some of them strange. But it will
work out to bless you and others if you will simply trust me and obey these
leadings as best you know how.

March Seventeenth

Jesus, looking at him, loved him and said, "You lack one thing; go, sell what you own, and give the money to the poor, and you will have treasure in heaven; then come, follow me." When he heard this, he was shocked and went away grieving, for he had many possessions.
—Mark 10:21–22

My child, do not close your ears and your mind to my voice out of fear of what I shall say to you! Have I not shown you my mercy at all times? There is no "unhappy surprise" awaiting you in what I shall say. My desire for you is that you outgrow the underlying fear and nameless dread which has plagued you all your life. Your sins are forgiven—all of them—by my shed blood on the cross. There is no condemnation awaiting you, even though you will need to confess and repent of any sin I convict you of. I say to you what I said in the Gospel again and again: your sins are forgiven! It is not my will that you linger in morbid concentration on your wrongness. Rather, my heart is gladdened by your thanksgiving, praise, and joy—and by your confidence in my eternal goodness. Keep listening for my word and plant yourself more surely on the firm foundation.

March Eighteenth

The LORD has done great things for us, and we rejoiced.
—Psalm 126:3

Your prayer is heard, my child, your prayer is heard. The desire you express is not yours, but the gift of my Spirit. Flesh recoils at the prospect of its mortality. The spirit within yearns to be clothed with immortality. Cultivate the spirit within. Deny the flesh its grasping, clinging—its fearful demands to be pampered, loved, considered. Fight the battle in the strength I shall give and be wholehearted in it. Call to mind, in the heat of battle, what great things I have done for you. I have taken your small, puny faith, and the steps you have taken in faith, and enlarged them beyond anything you can see. Only I know the extent of my blessing, but you can know enough to strengthen you and arm you when the adversary comes in like a flood. Play the man, my child. Your prayer is heard.

March Nineteenth

Hold to the standard of sound teaching that you have heard from me,
in the faith and love that are in Christ Jesus.
—2 Timothy 1:13

Guard well, my child, the life I have given you. The adversary is ever seeking ways to nullify and make havoc of your faith. You are no match for him without me, and you easily forget how dangerous it is to wander from the safe path. I warn you not to be presumptuous. I am your safety, your front guard and your rear guard. You are safe when you stay with me. That is how you guard the life I have given you.

March Twentieth

With joy you will draw water from the wells of salvation. And you will say in that day: Give thanks to the LORD, call on his name. . . .
—Isaiah 12:3–4a

"With joy you will draw water from the wells of salvation." The wells are deep and sometimes you must wait for the plumbing of the depths. The surface of your soul is like the surface of the sea—busily moving in many directions at the gusts of wind that blow on it. There is a restlessness that you must get past. Or change the picture, my child, and compare it to a dry and thirsty desert—unstable and shifting in many directions. So do not be discouraged that I require you to go deeper than the shifting sand, the restless sea. Quietness is in the depths. The water of salvation is plentiful and pure, but must be drawn from its source. Since most of your life is lived on the surface, it is all the more necessary that you take the time to go deep and tap the life-giving wells.

March Twenty-first

Because the LORD your God is a merciful God, he will neither abandon
you nor destroy you. . . .
—Deuteronomy 4:31a

Do not fear the path that I have laid out for you. Do not flinch at what I ask you to bear. You will not bear it alone. Lo, I am with you, my child, in every moment. I tell you this because I know you from your conception in your mother's womb. She, too, feared many things. Your feeling of aloneness and abandonment are made more intense by your sin. The fear you feel is a punishment for your rebellion against my love. All rebellion is against my love, because I, the Lord, am love. That is the essence of my nature. You are a creature, a creation of my love. When you understand that simple truth, you will know freedom from fear. You will know that I will never abandon you. Never. That is my promise.

March Twenty-second

Day and night without ceasing they sing, "Holy, holy, holy, the Lord God
Almighty, who was and is and is to come."
—Revelation 4:8b–9

Abiding in me is the key to peace. Your heart can know no peace when you
wander into the world. I am abiding in you, as I have promised. That is a reality—even though you are seldom aware of it. If you would practice living
in my presence you would know greater peace and freedom, for I am here.
Abiding in me is your half of the equation. Blessings can and will multiply
when you make that choice. It is the key to peace.

March Twenty-third

*. . . break up your fallow ground; for it is time to seek the LORD,
that he may come and rain righteousness upon you.*
—Hosea 10:12b

Feast on my Word. This is the true food for your soul. The words that I speak to you are spirit, and they are life. By this I mean that they become sustenance for your spirit, and life for your soul. I make words alive by my Spirit so that they become expressions of my Word.

You need to trust, to learn to trust, the living word that comes to you. My word comes to break up the hard, fallow ground of your heart. Do you not see it? Is it not happening? But there is much work still to be done. I am the restorer of divisions. I am he who breaks down walls of separation.

March Twenty-fourth

My child, if your heart is wise, my heart too will be glad.
—Proverbs 23:15

Wandering about and lingering in doubt, you wait and hesitate. I, too, wait to be gracious. I do not delay in coming to you. The delay is yours, my child. The enemy is ever ready to seek an entrance into your thoughts—interfering with our appointed meeting. The loss is yours, for I am ready to lead you into a more stable and productive relationship. I am not playing spiritual games with you. I rebuke you, my child, for your lack of willingness to fight harder against this lethargy and uncommitted attitude.

Come to me expecting to be spoken to like an adult. Come to me expecting to speak your need, but not to wallow in it.

March Twenty-fifth

The jar of meal was not emptied, neither did the jug of oil fail,
according to the word of the LORD that he spoke by Elijah.
—I Kings 17:16

My goodness never fails. If my people would only trust me more, they would see the unending stream of mercy flowing like a mighty river, an unending supply. Your life is a testimony to the surprising ways I use to supply the needs of my children. From the day you gave your heart to me, the cruse of oil has never run dry. Through lean times and fat, you have never lacked what you needed. I have fed you with the finest wheat.

Go over my promises in your mind and praise my faithfulness! Surprise yourself anew at the remembrance of my goodness. There is a pattern here that I want you to recognize. This, too, is a part of the blessing I give you—the joy and trust that such memories bring.

March Twenty-sixth

I am confident of this, that the one who began a good work among you
will bring it to completion by the day of Jesus Christ.
—Philippians 1:6

In the safety of my care you may rest your soul. No harm can reach you here
where my power and protection prevail. You have often looked beyond that
safety, fantasizing how much better life would be apart from the narrowness
of my way. You have robbed yourself of much peace that was available to
you.

My work is still going on in your soul. Yes, it is repair work, and therefore slow and painstaking. But it is *my* work, and it must be done according
to my design, not yours. If my ways seem strange, recall often my tender
mercies. Stand on solid ground, look up, believe, and you will see the glory
of God.

March Twenty-seventh

*And my God will fully satisfy every need of yours according
to his riches in glory in Christ Jesus.*
—Philippians 4:19

My wisdom is not of this world. It seems foolish to the mind of the natural
man. Yet I continually prove its value to those who find it. You still have too
much reliance on human wisdom and too little trust in my wisdom. You are
still too cautious in relinquishing *everything* to me. I will do you no harm;
I am your Savior, not your destroyer!

March Twenty-eighth

From the rising of the sun to its setting the name
of the LORD is to be praised.
—Psalm 113:3

It is good to wait in my presence. You are being blessed and fed by my Spirit, even when you hear no words. It is good to keep trusting when your prayers are delayed. You have been long in coming to this place, and there is still much ground to reclaim. You have built a fortress around your mind, and trusted in your own thoughts and opinions rather than in me. They failed you when great need arose, and you were faced with your inability to help. I have not failed you, but you forfeited much peace by your choices. It is good to wait in my presence. This too is part of my work to help you regain and reclaim lost ground.

March Twenty-ninth

. . . for whenever I am weak, then I am strong.
—2 Corinthians 12:10b

I have seen your affliction. The wounds and scars of your soul are not hidden from me. "I am the LORD who heals you" (Exodus 15:26d). That is my gracious and self–chosen work within you, my child. It is my work, and yours to accept with faith and gratitude. Let no thoughts from the adversary bring doubts in your mind about my purpose and my power. I do not work as humans work, and the process is largely hidden from your view. This is where I call on you to fight doubt and discouragement and to exercise faith in me. I give you this part of the battle out of my love for you. Don't try to *understand*, but stand *under* the mercy which covers you.

March Thirtieth

I will pray with the spirit, but I will pray with the mind also; I will
sing praise with the spirit, but I will sing with the mind also.
—I Corinthians 14:15b

Pray with your eyes open. Pray with your heart open. Pray with your ears open—open to me and my word. Pray with a song in your heart, a song of deliverance, a song of thanksgiving. Prepare yourself to be in my company with repentance and confession—covered with my forgiveness and the mantle of my mercy. Thus we can have sweet fellowship together—a blessing to you and a joy to my fatherly heart. Put away fear of offending me as long as you do what I have told you. A lively, living trust is more pleasing than groveling at my feet. Enter my presence with thanksgiving, and "approach the throne of grace with boldness" (Hebrews 4:16a). I welcome you, my beloved child.

March Thirty-first

. . . the mother of Jesus said to him, "They have no wine."
And Jesus said to her, "Woman, what concern is that to you and me?
My hour has not yet come."
—John 2:3b–4

My promises are not in vain. You have ample proof of this, my child, in the answers to your prayers. I want you to exercise your faith in my word. I want you to leave behind the caution and hesitation that are expressions of doubt. Move along the path I have laid out for you, and I will help you claim new ground. My promises are not in vain.

APRIL

O for a closer walk with God,
 A calm and heavenly frame,
A light to shine upon the road
 That leads me to the Lamb!

Return, O holy Dove, return,
 Sweet messenger of rest!
I hate the sins that made Thee mourn
 And drove Thee from my breast.

The dearest idol I have known,
 Whate'er that idol be,
Help me to tear it from Thy throne,
 And worship only Thee.

So shall my walk be close with God,
 Calm and serene my frame;
So purer light shall mark the road
 That leads me to the Lamb.

—William Cowper, 1731–1800

April First

All people are grass, their constancy is like the flower of the field.
The grass withers, the flower fades, . . . but the word of our
God will stand forever.
—Isaiah 40:6b–8

The Word of the Lord endures—forever.

Before me the generations rise and pass away. I call them to myself. Eternity is little in your thoughts and plans. The immediate and near future occupy your mind. Yet I have called you, and do call you, to be with me in eternity. Can you not see how that changes the perspective on *every* earthly circumstance and relationship? Oh, the blindness of my people! You scurry about and worry about these little, trivial, passing things—and neglect the one thing needful—preparing for your eternal destiny. I have given my Word—and it stands forever. Do not depart from it to the left or to the right. Seek my face. Seek my blessing. Trust me in all the relationships of your life. They are in my keeping. Sickness, separation—and death—cannot destroy what I keep safe. I know when to give and when to withhold. I am with you for good.

April Second

. . . and live in love, as Christ loved us and gave himself for us,
a fragrant offering and sacrifice to God.
—Ephesians 5:2

Begin and end the day with me, my child, and let the hours between be a walking together in love. Remember that you are my servant, and you are responsible to spend your hours in my service. Your life is not your own. You have been bought with a great price. Do not take it back to yourself, for that is robbery. Learn what it means to be a purchased possession—a ransomed soul. Live out your freedom in the light of who I am and who you are. Begin and end the day with me, my child, and let all the hours between be a walking together in love.

April Third

O taste and see that the LORD is good. . . .
—Psalm 34:8a

To taste, you must take the food into yourself. Taste is a way of trying, of testing the goodness of the food. In like manner, the tasting, the testing of spiritual food is a necessary part of your experience. You have "tasted" many unhealthy substitutes, and your soul was wounded—harmed—by taking in corrupting and tainted substances. The effects have been serious but not fatal, because my sovereign purpose overruled your foolish choices.

Taste and see the food that I supply—the nourishing and healing food of my Word and Spirit. Doubt not that I am the bread of life—and that I stand the "taste test"!

April Fourth

"I am the light of the world. Whoever follows me will never walk in darkness but will have the light of life."
—John 8:12b

According to your faith let it be to you, O you of little faith! Your lack of faith leaves your soul shriveled and bent—for a whole dimension is under-developed. Your reasoning and doubt is over-developed. And the distortion hinders your walk with me. I have given you ample reason to trust me with your whole heart. I have given you more than you have asked or thought. So the time is here for faith to flourish and catch up—will you allow it to happen?

April Fifth

*For those whom he foreknew he also predestined to be
conformed to the image of his Son. . . .*
—Romans 8:29a

The spirit of prayer is my gift to you. It is the means by which you open the doors of your heart, the gates of your soul, to me. I will come into that guarded place only when you open the gate to me. So when the Holy Spirit moves you to open the gates, do so heartily and expectantly.

A little child, seeking its mother's breast, is not distracted easily. Its hunger drives it to a single-mindedness and a concentration that you will do well to emulate. Here at the throne of grace there is nourishment, refreshment, and guidance for your daily needs. I do not want you to miss the riches of grace, the showers of blessing, I have prepared for you.

April Sixth

But you have come to Mount Zion and to the city of the living God, the heavenly Jerusalem, and to innumerable angels in festal gathering. . . .
—Hebrews 12:22

"The place on which you are standing is holy ground" (Exodus 3:5b). All ground is holy when it becomes a place of meeting. I am always with you, and yet there needs to be these places and times where my glory breaks through to you. You could not bear yet to live constantly in the vision of my glory. Your eyes and your heart are not yet prepared. But these glimpses are foretastes, and they are my gift to you.

April Seventh

"I am the resurrection and the life. Those who believe in me,
even though they die, will live, and everyone who lives and
believes in me will never die."
—John 11:25b–26

This is my word for you today: take heed to everything I say—not just in this morning hour, but throughout the day. I will guide you and help you, my child, if you will keep a listening ear. You cannot chart the day without me, and you are not strong enough to stand against your adversaries without me. Do not overestimate your strength nor underestimate that of the enemy. You have ample evidence to show what a weak pawn you are in his hand when you separate yourself from my loving care. So do not be a foolish child who despises the father's instruction, but be wise in your weakness, and keep listening to me.

April Eighth

But grow in the grace and knowledge of our Lord and Savior Jesus
Christ. To him be the glory both now and to the day of eternity.
—2 Peter 3:18

Becoming. You are becoming that for which I created and redeemed you.
You are becoming what you are not yet. You are becoming what only I can
see. When your love for me is perfected, you will have no fear of me. When
you know as you are known, there will be no need to hide. Where my image
and my plan have become what you are, then fullness of joy will be yours. In
the meantime, my child, press toward the mark. Keep becoming.

April Ninth

". . . let your light shine before others, so that they may see your good works and give glory to your Father in heaven."
—Matthew 5:16

The light on your path never goes out. It is always enough to guide you along the chosen way. If your way seems dark and uncertain, find out where you have willfully chosen another path. My way is not always easy—but it is always good.

I have compassion on you and your family. Much suffering has been experienced in all of you. I know your case and my work is not yet complete. My glory shall yet be revealed, so do not lose heart!

April Tenth

. . . but those who wait for the LORD shall renew their strength. . . .
—Isaiah 40:31a

The clamor of this world has dulled your ears to the sound of my voice. I still speak as I did to Elijah in the "still, small voice." As long as your heart is pulled after worldly delights, the dullness will persist. Only as and if you center more and more on my will and my concerns will you find it easy to hear.

I counsel you once again, do not lose heart. Do not forget that "those who wait for the LORD shall renew their strength." And they will improve their hearing as well.

April Eleventh

Consider your own call, brothers and sisters: not many of you were wise
by human standards, not many were powerful, not many were of noble
birth. But God chose what is foolish in the world to shame the wise. . . .
—1 Corinthians 1:26–27a

I have not called you to greatness as the world counts greatness. Your great-ness is to be plowed under, the seed that falls into the ground that life may spring forth. My life in you requires a corresponding death in yours. This is done in part by the denial of your craving for recognition and applause.

The glory I offer you will not feed your sin-appetite. When I lead you "from one degree of glory to another" (2 Corinthians 3:18c) you will know and recognize that the glory is mine and the blessing of it is more than all the world could give.

April Twelfth

*"I tell you, there is joy in the presence of the angels of
God over one sinner who repents."*
—Luke 15:10

My dear child, put away vain thoughts and regrets. I know all your way—and
I have never abandoned you, no matter how far you strayed from the straight
path of my will. Let this be a cause of rejoicing and thanksgiving, even as you
mourn the folly of your self-directed course. Repentance is forward-looking,
not backward-gazing. I am God, and I still restore the locust-eaten years.
Your great need, my child, is more faith in me.

April Thirteenth

He is able to deal gently with the ignorant and wayward,
since he himself is subject to weakness. . . .
—Hebrews 5:2

Today I am leading you along a path you have not walked before. To your eye, it may seem familiar and ordinary. But you have not lived "here" before—for each new moment is just that: new. Do not allow the ordinariness of the day to obscure its true reality, my child.

April Fourteenth

Like obedient children, do not be conformed to the
desires that you formerly had in ignorance.
—I Peter 1:14

My dear child, walking in obedience is done a step at a time. It is not yours to seek the long view, for you would then be tempted to seize control of your path, thinking you knew the way. I am the Way, and by the simple act of obeying step by step, you will arrive at the goal. Build up your own faith in this way, and encourage other fainthearted souls to do the same. Strong faith comes from pressing on when the outcome seems uncertain.

April Fifteenth

"So I tell you, whatever you ask for in prayer, believe
that you have received it, and it will be yours."
—Mark 11:24

In the book of remembrance, write: "Thus far the LORD has helped us" (1 Samuel 7:12). In the book of remembrance, recall my acts of mercy. Let the memory of past mercies cheer you in hard places. As I have been faithful of old, I will not cease to be faithful now. Your way is laid out before you. My plan unfolds day by day. Thus far I have helped you, and today I am the same.

April Sixteenth

"Where, O death, is your victory? Where, O death, is your sting?" The sting of death is sin, and the power of sin is the law. But thanks be to God, who gives us the victory through our Lord Jesus Christ.
—I Corinthians 15:55–57

O my child, hear my good word to you today. Death has been defeated. It no longer has dominion over my people. I am the Lord, and I choose how to call each of my own to me. Death is a door—a door out and a door in. For my children it is a door out of suffering and pain, with all the uncertainties they feel in this earthly life; a door into the life I have prepared for you. That is enough for you—if you will remain close to me. You do not need to know more, just that through that door I will be waiting for you.

April Seventeenth

*How does God's love abide in anyone who has the world's goods
and sees a brother or sister in need and yet refuses help?*
—1 John 3:17

This is my word today: compassion. Pray for compassion! You have an unmerciful heart. You rejoice at the discomfiture of those who have offended you. You place yourself "above" them in your mind, forgetting who and what you are in truth. Your harsh and unmerciful attitude puts a wall—a strong barrier—between us. Little wonder that you are then plagued with fear and anxiety. I am your peace; I am the place of tranquility and quietness—but an unmerciful heart cannot dwell there.

April Eighteenth

Not one of all the good promises that the LORD had made
to the house of Israel had failed; all came to pass.
—Joshua 21:45

My child, do not doubt my love. Put away the accusing thoughts that rise in your mind. These are not from me, but from the enemy camp. Rehearse often the footprints of my deliverances and my provision. Trace the outlines of my mercy.

The supply of manna never ran short for my people. It has never run short for you. There have always been the angels of my presence to aid and provide what you needed. The more you realize this, the more your gratitude will displace your doubts.

April Nineteenth

I dwell in the high and holy place, and also with those who are contrite and humble in spirit, to revive the spirit of the humble, and to revive the heart of the contrite.
—Isaiah 57:15b

The broken and contrite heart is the work of my grace. Blessed are they who weep over their sin and shed tears of joy over my mercy. Blessed are they who find the secret place when we commune Spirit to spirit. Many call on me in distress, but few yearn for such times of meeting. Guard well this privilege, my child. Never take it for granted or treat it as casual or ordinary. It is part of my preparatory work on your soul.

April Twentieth

. . . ponder it on your beds, and be silent.
—Psalm 4:4b

"Be still and know that I am God" (Psalm 46:10). Be still, for in the stillness you will come to know what you cannot learn in your impatient movement. How seldom you are ever quiet within! Even when you are doing nothing, there is still strain and tension, indicating an absence of the stillness. Stilling the murmurs, the dissatisfaction, the jealousies, the hurts, and the vain ambitions—these you can do with my help. They will not go away without your active choice against them. Stillness will follow, but you must claim it by rejecting these roots of unrest in your soul. Be still and you will know.

April Twenty-first

Therefore the LORD waits to be gracious to you;
therefore he will rise up to show mercy to you.
—Isaiah 30:18a

My dear child, this truly is the throne of grace. It is purely my grace alone that makes these meetings possible. You have neither earned nor deserved the privilege I have given you. Magnify my grace in your heart. Put down any feelings or thoughts that you are "special." It is enough that I love you, include you in the circle of my little ones, have pity on you, and convey my truth to your soul. That is reason enough for an eternity of gratitude on your part.

April Twenty-second

Draw near to God, and he will draw near to you.
—James 4:8a

Call upon me, and I will answer you. Draw near to me, and I will draw near to you. This is ever my word and my promise. I know your frame and your weakness. I know the difficulty you have in keeping your thoughts on me. I know all about you—more, much more than you know about yourself. So come to me in your brokenness, your failure to measure up, your baseless fears. I will not turn you away, because I love you. You will come to know me as I reveal my love to you. Call upon me and I *will* answer you.

April Twenty-third

. . . no evil shall befall you, no scourge come near your tent.
Psalm 91:10

"A thousand may fall at your side, ten thousand at your right hand, but it will not come near you" (Psalm 91:7). Because each child of mine is my peculiar and particular care, this saying is true. My protection is over you, to keep you in all your ways. This is not an excuse for presumption or pride, but an opportunity for humble gratitude.

Make the best of the days I have given you to live. Do not waste them in idleness or despair. Play the man! Gird yourself for battle against the enemy's assaults—and honor me in your victories.

April Twenty-fourth

And the peace of God, which surpasses all understanding,
will guard your hearts and your minds in Christ Jesus.
Philippians 4:7

The peace that surpasses understanding is an active power, an active still-ness, which stirs hope and joy even in the midst of trouble. As long as you are in the world there will be trouble, tribulation, trials. These trials are not to destroy you, nor to dampen your faith in me, but are to purify your soul and wean it from its captivity to a passing world. Your soul has not yet become firmly attached to that which cannot be shaken, so with every blow to its false security a choice is open to choose the better part.

I know your fears—from your own weakness and of what might lie ahead for you. I call you now to trust yourself to my care, to lean on my strength, to rest on my promise. Your fears will subside; they are not om-nipotent—I am. They are subject to me and to your obedience to me. As your love for me grows, they will diminish. Peace replaces panic. I, the Lord, reign.

April Twenty-fifth

. . . a bruised reed he will not break, and a dimly
burning wick he will not quench.
—Isaiah 42:3a

Yes, I am your Lord and your God. I give you life and breath moment by moment. You are entirely in my care. I touch not only the mountain but hearts, setting them aflame with my love.

Nourish the flame, my child. Vain regret is not repentance. Keep open to the breath of my Spirit and open to my love. Obey the gentle commands and become more sensitive to my ways. Be strong and of good courage, and I will strengthen your heart. I am able to do exceedingly beyond all your poor mind can ask or think.

April Twenty-sixth

. . . you are not your own . . . For you were bought with a price;
therefore glorify God in your body.
—I Corinthians 6:19b–20

Pray to me, my child, pray to me. You are still prayerless through much of
your day. You still have not learned the secret of continual fellowship with
me, and you walk through much of your day cut off, as it were, from me. I am
still with you, but your life would be much more fruitful if you learned the
secret of praying without ceasing. It is an attitude—not an activity. It is possible even in busy hours to maintain the spirit of prayer. I have told you to
turn every circumstance and care into prayer. I repeat my words. Turn *every-*
thing into prayer—thanksgiving or petition, praise or intercession. Practice!
Repent of your past passivity and spiritual laziness! Awake to the possibilities
I hold before you, and engage in this struggle. Signs still follow those who
follow my word.

April Twenty-seventh

"From everyone to whom much has been given,
much will be required. . . ."
—Luke 12:48b

You are my beloved child. I know you and see you with all your faults and sin. I have redeemed you. You are mine. But I will not tolerate your sin and rebellion against me. That I will deal with in justice and mercy.

Do not withdraw from me in pride and fear. Let my gracious words assure you that my love is greater than your sin, greater than your need. There is no shortage of grace and mercy as we walk together. Smile at your foes, for they will not prevail.

April Twenty-eighth

"Call on me in the day of trouble; I will deliver you,
and you shall glorify me."
—Psalm 50:15

Call on me, my child, and I will answer you. Not only do my sheep hear my voice, but I hear the voice of my sheep. Do not marvel that among the millions of voices on earth, I hear and recognize the voices of my own. You think this is presumptuous—to count yourself among "my own." It is only that you are realizing in greater depth and intensity what it means to be claimed by my love. Leave the mysteries to me, child. Quiet your soul as a little child. My Presence now can quiet every fear.

Let your situation work my purpose out in your inner life, and it will bring forth fruit in your works. First things first.

April Twenty-ninth

"For I also am a man under authority, with soldiers under me;
and I say to one, 'Go' and he goes, and to another, 'Come,' and he
comes, and to my slave, 'Do this,' and the slave does it."
—Matthew 8:9

I want you to learn to move boldly and quickly when I speak to you. You are beset by many misgivings and doubts, and these hinder your growth in me. Those who would walk with me must learn this secret, for it transfers the "control" out of your hands. I know the fears that come into your mind, but I tell you this: your hesitation and reasoning are more harmful than any mistake you would make in obeying what you believe to be my will. Avoiding one error, you fall into a greater one. Learn, my child, that I am not playing games with you.

April Thirtieth

You shall put the mercy seat on the top of the ark. . . . There I
will meet with you. . . . from above the mercy seat. . . .
—Exodus 25:21a–22a

My dear child, comfort your heart at my mercy seat. Here there is a foretaste
of the blessedness that I have prepared for you and all my children. Here
there is a breakthrough from the dullness and denseness that characterizes
most of your life. That is the wellspring of your tears—the unguardedness
of your heart. Do not be surprised that no great "words" or revelations come
in these meetings. You do not need them. What you need, my child, is the
assurance of my love and care. I see you trying to reach out and make
connections in different directions—children, family, friends—and for the
most part they fail you. But that is because they cannot supply what only I
can give. Remember the word, "You open your hand, satisfying the desire
of every living thing" (Psalm 145:16). One thing must precede that: the
shaping of your desire away from destructive ends. When your heart is at
peace, yearning for that which is withheld ceases. All things are yours when
your heart is at peace.

So come to this seat often—this mercy seat. I have promised in my
holy Word that I will meet with you here. Learn here the secret of my love.

MAY

I sought the Lord, and afterward I knew
    he moved my soul to seek him, seeking
        me;
It was not I that found, O Savior true;
    No, I was found of Thee.

Thou didst reach forth thy hand and mine
        enfold;
    I walked and sank not on the storm-
        vexed sea;
'Twas not so much that I on thee took hold
    As Thou, dear Lord, on me.

I find, I walk, I love, but O the whole
    Of love is but my answer, Lord, to thee!
For thou wast long beforehand with
        my soul;
    Always thou lovedst me.

—Anon., c. 1880

May First

Happy are those who find wisdom, and those who get understanding. . . .
Her ways are ways of pleasantness, and all her paths are peace.
—Proverbs 3:13, 17

Walk in my ways today, my child. My ways are ways of blessedness and peace. Mine is a safe way—surrounded by all the protection you need from the enemy.

Leave to me the concerns about the future—your future and that of those you love. The future is in my hands, and you can safely entrust it to me.

Redeem the time. The days are short and much has been wasted in your past years. But it is enough—and I will be with you to claim the present for my purposes. Be of good cheer!

May Second

"And now, O LORD, what do I wait for? My hope is in you."
—Psalm 39:7

Hope! Hope! Hope! Hope is my gift in the interim time—when your heart is turned toward me. There is no place for hopelessness in your relationship with me, for the future—your future—is in my hand. Your sins of worry and fear are like acids that eat away at the hope I give you. Hope is like a beckoning light before you, and is meant to encourage you when things are difficult. It is a precious gift. Do not waste it!

No one can thwart my sovereign will. That is why hope is a trustworthy guide. You do not need to understand all mysteries, how I shall accomplish my will—either in you or in others. But you do need to claim and cherish and *nourish* the gift of hope.

Bid others to be of good cheer. Too much fear darkens the hearts of my people. Bid them to be of good cheer! The darkness cannot prevail because the true light has come. Become a people of praise.

May Third

For thus said the Lord GOD, the Holy One of Israel:
In returning and rest you shall be saved;
in quietness and in trust shall be your strength. . . .
—Isaiah 30:15

Quietness is difficult for you because you have yet to learn to direct your thoughts and keep them on me. You love the wanderings of your mind and easily let them carry you away.

Stillness is a state of rest in my presence. It is my gift to you when you are ready for it. Much of the turmoil you experience is the fruit of your own choices and the consequences of your wandering mind. Instead of wandering, my child, try *wondering*.

May Fourth

He has made everything suitable for its time. . . .
—Ecclesiastes 3:11a

The beauty of this world does not compare with the glory of the next. It is, however, a foretaste, just as the peace I give here is a foretaste of my kingdom. Enjoy the beauty here. It is my gift to you. I put the hunger for it in your heart, and it is I who fulfills that hunger.

Embrace the life to which I have called you. Do not question my purposes, for they are hidden from you for your good. Your walk will have many thorns—but always there will be beauty—and the thorns are protective against that which would destroy. O my child, let the beauty of my world open your eyes more eagerly to the beauty of my life, my kingdom. You have only begun to touch the hem of my garment, the edges of my ways.

May Fifth

. . . we who have taken refuge might be strongly encouraged to
seize the hope set before us. We have this hope, a sure and . . .
steadfast anchor of the soul.
—Hebrews 6:18b–19a

Cling to my cross. It is the anchor of your soul. Wild thoughts, ideas, temptations—all would dash you to pieces. Here, only here, is your safety. It is the Rock of Ages—and in it there is safety through every storm.

Cling to my cross. For there you know for certain that your only claim on me is my sovereign love. You did not create it—it was before you. You do not control it or destroy it—for I am God. But clinging here, you can keep a fresh awareness of the relationship between us. It is based not on merit but on grace.

You are a very insecure soul—never fully trusting for more than a moment. Your faith is still weak and puny—and far from the robust health I will for it. Your past trials have had some results—but O, my child, how much more you could have learned from my goodness!

May Sixth

I am about to do a new thing; now it springs forth,
do you not perceive it?
—Isaiah 43:19a

My dear child, I am writing a new word upon your heart. Heretofore you have never fully accepted my love in its simplicity. Anxiety and fear have shut the door against my offered presence. Sin and rebellion within, then, have wreaked havoc in the place where I would have reigned. Confusion and misdirection prevailed where order and progress could have been manifest. You know in part some of the pain and distress that resulted.

You weep now. Others have wept for you—and prayed that your eyes might be open to the truth. Do not close your heart to me. Do not let pride shut out my abiding, guiding presence. I am here to bless you, and through you to bless others. When the evening comes there shall be light.

May Seventh

*I want you to know, beloved, that what has happened to
me has actually helped to spread the gospel. . . .*
—Philippians 1:12

Your disappointments of the past were but steps along the path that led
you back to me. Know that I withhold no good thing from those who
love me. But when your desires and ambitions led you in contrary ways, I
wisely cut them off to safe limits—having always in view that which would
ultimately satisfy your deepest desire. That is my wisdom and mercy—it
is always in operation, unseen and unrecognized by my children. So your
disappointments become inconsequential—except that they are signposts
of my overruling hand of mercy on you. Believe this, my child, and count
it all joy. There is no loss—no ultimate loss—to you if you will accept my
higher gift—the treasure of my love in the secret place of your heart. So few
find it! Be one of them.

May Eighth

The LORD is my shepherd, I shall not want.
—Psalm 23:1

By flowing streams I lead my flock. They shall not be left in the desert of desire. My living water I supply, that in their thirst they shall not die. Be refreshed at the river of life, my child, and know it ever flows from my throne. Your thirst can never be satisfied elsewhere, but here and here alone. These waters offer cleansing, as well, so stop, and wash, and drink, and live.

May Ninth

The friendship of the LORD is for those who fear him,
and he makes his covenant known to them.
—Psalm 25:14

Be still! Be still, my child! Let anxious thoughts subside, and old accusing ones die. I am the One who brought you safe thus far—I am the One who overruled the raging seas of your ambitions and emotions. I am the One who steered you into a safe haven. Be still! Rejoice! Rejoice at the remembrance of my holiness. Rejoice at the remembrance of my deliverances. Rejoice that you are known and loved.

Repent! Let the conviction of my Holy Spirit move you to abandon the strongholds of sin in your heart. Let my light penetrate the places of deception and falsehood—that the truth may free you more and more to live in harmony with me.

May Tenth

No good thing does the LORD withhold from those who walk uprightly. O
LORD of hosts, happy is everyone who trusts in you.
—Psalm 84:11b–12

My ear is always open to the cry of my children. None calls to me in vain.
Your cries and prayers are heard and laid up—deposited in my heart—and I
will not forget them. I have committed myself to be a prayer-hearer. You have
come late to the place of prayer.

Although you learned early that I answer prayer, you did not grow in
true prayer. For you it was a cry in a tight spot. It is meant to be more—
much more than a cry for help in desperation. Yet even that I do not despise,
because I know it can lead on beyond itself. True prayer still takes place in
the secret place where we can commune as Friend with friend. Treasure it,
my child, and grow in it.

May Eleventh

I blessed the Most High, and praised and honored the one who lives forever.
—Daniel 4:34b

Keep praising! Praise brings light into your darkness and health into your sickness. Keep praising! You are blessed even as you bless. You are built up even as you remember and extol my works. My joy is fulfilled in your joy. My will is fulfilled in the harmony between your spirit and my Spirit. That harmony is the music of the spheres. That harmony is the echo of my creative plan. You touch only its edges, but even that is not to be despised. Keep praising. There are mysteries here that you have not begun to comprehend.

May Twelfth

I want to know Christ and the power of his resurrection and the sharing
of his sufferings by becoming like him in his death. . . .
—Philippians 3:10

Avoiding suffering is avoiding me, for I am there for you. I do not delight
in seeing my children in pain. I do not willingly afflict my children. But
you know, my child, that I have suffered for you, and that those who love
me are given to share in my sufferings. You do not, you cannot, understand
this with your natural mind. Only the experience itself can reveal what I
am saying.

You have not been a willing participant in my suffering, and have
sought various ways to avoid it. Only my persistent love that would not let
you go prevailed—and you see a little clearer the secrets hidden there. There is
no cause for fear—only faithful assent to that which I allow. It will be alright.

May Thirteenth

Therefore, since we are surrounded by so great a cloud of witnesses, let us also lay aside every weight and the sin that clings so closely, and let us run with perseverance the race that is set before us, looking unto Jesus the pioneer and perfector of our faith. . . .
—Hebrews 12:1–2a

The mystery of the communion of saints is the mystery of prayer. It is the opening up of the barrier that now separates those who are earth-bound and those who have "made it home." Remembering those who have gone ahead is part of this communion. Keeping the memory alive—for generations—is an important part. You are all bound together in my love, and you are called to be a praying people. I allow for many mistakes in your struggle to understand, for I know how limited your capacities are. But I want you to keep seeking, knocking, and asking, that your capacity may grow, and that you participate more freely in this blessed communion.

I woke up this morning thinking that Dick & I would make it to the finish line. Then saw the above scripture on running with perseverence the race that is set before us!

May Fourteenth

But I will hope continually, and will praise you yet more and more.
—Psalm 71:14

This is my word today: anxiety has no place in our relationship. Your anxiety is rooted in lack of faith in my overarching, prevailing goodness. I have given assurances and have fulfilled promises. Let your eyes focus on that reality and turn away from vain imaginations. This is a time for faith. Believe as you have never believed before—let yourself believe and do not hold back!

May Fifteenth

*Blessed be the God and Father of our Lord Jesus Christ who has blessed
us with every spiritual blessing in the heavenly places. . . .*
—Ephesians 1:3

I bless you, my child, because you are mine. This is not because of your merits or achievements—for you know they are not worthy of my blessing. No, it is because my favor rests on you, and I have chosen to make you one of mine, that the blessing comes.

You are worried and anxious about many small things. They pass into eternity in a moment. You fear what might lie ahead for you—but do you doubt my blessing? Away with your infantile preoccupations! The hour is late. Enter into the blessing I am giving you *today.* Do not harden your heart against me in fear.

May Sixteenth

Then the angel showed me . . . [o]n either side of the river is the tree of life with its twelve kinds of fruit, producing its fruit each month. . . .
—Revelation 22:1a & 2a

The tree of life yields its fruit in season. The cross blossoms with new beauty when you come to me with your repentance. Far deeper than you can know, I plant the seed of my word in you. Hidden from your eyes, the growth *is* taking place. Your despair and your feeling depressed are merely the products of your unbelief. Put away sorrow, put away anxiety, put away the hurt and jealousy you feel—and rejoice that the tree will bear its fruit each month. Have I not told you?

May Seventeenth

Do not fret——it leads only to evil.
—Psalm 37:8b

Do not fret about situations you cannot change. It is part of your acceptance of your weakness and impotence in situations that are beyond your control. You have good words for others. Apply them to yourself and focus on the responsibilities I have given you. In your obedience to these responsibilities you will be blessed, and you will be a blessing. Do not waste yourself in fretting.

May Eighteenth

Take delight in the LORD, and he will give you the desires of your heart.
—Psalm 37:4

Delight yourself in me, my child; and know that such delight is your true inheritance. My joy and my peace are gifts I delight to share. The world is a sad place. There is much suffering, pain, and sorrow. Yet there is also, intermingled with it, a joy to be found. My purpose is still unfolding, and there are many evidences of it to those with eyes to see. So there is good reason to delight yourself in me.

May Nineteenth

Jesus Christ is the same yesterday and today and forever.
—Hebrews 13:8

My dear child, I have not changed, I am still the same—yesterday, today, and forever. I counsel you to ground your soul in this truth. Clouds may temporarily hide the sun but they do not *change* the sun. So with my love for you. Clouds may hide it for a time, but I do not change and my love is ever toward you and with you. Rest in the reality of it.

May Twentieth

Thus says the LORD: Stand at the crossroads, and look,
and ask for the ancient paths, where the good way lies;
and walk in it, and find rest for your souls.
—Jeremiah 6:16

You are walking a new path—and yet an old path. It was offered to you long ago, but you were not ready to receive it. In these intervening years you have wandered far from that path—sometimes very near to the pit of destruction. Only my grace and fatherly hand kept you back. The many crooks and turns in your pilgrimage were the results of these two forces—your blindness and my grace. Remember, my child, that I am afflicted in the affliction of my children, and I do not willingly cause grief to those I love. Yet I use the grief and the affliction for my purposes. But it is my will that you walk this path. Fear not. It is a good path, and I am your protection in it. Have I not proven that through these long years? I will bless you and make you a blessing. Leave that to me. That is my promise.

May Twenty-first

. . . to provide for those that mourn in Zion—to give them a garland instead of ashes, the oil of gladness instead of mourning, the mantle of praise instead of a faint spirit.
—Isaiah 61:3a

I come to you laden with gifts, gifts of my love. I am the Divine Giver, and it is my pleasure to bestow upon my children the gift of my love. There is the gift of understanding and light—as the light of my truth penetrates the darkness of your doubt and fearful hesitation. There is the gift of faith that enables you to receive and write these words. And, of course, my child, the gift of repentance, for you still have great need of it.

My hand is open toward those who love me, and my ear is open to their cry. Fear not! Your prayer is heard—and the answer is prepared ahead of time. You are still too inexperienced and untrustworthy to be told more than this. Sometimes my gift is the patience to wait. In the meantime, you can praise my faithfulness.

May Twenty-second

O that my people would listen to me, that Israel would walk in my ways!
—Psalm 81:13

Trust my words more implicitly. Give up your time and energy-wasting reasoning. Be willing, my child, to be foolish in the eyes of others in order to be wise in my sight. Remember that the world around you still walks in darkness, even though the light has come. Its reasoning and wisdom are folly. Do not be seduced by them.

Trust my words more implicitly and walk with me.

May Twenty-third

. . . with everlasting love I will have compassion on you,
says the LORD, your Redeemer.
—Isaiah 54:8b

My child, my child, know this about me: my love is unchangeable. It knows no waxing or waning. Your emotions are unstable—they wax warm and cold. But you are held in my unchanging love—even when you cannot feel it or recognize it. I have told you before that I am the Light in the midst of darkness—for in me there is no shadow of turning. So when your way is dark, turn to me as once you did to your earthly father. All is well, and secure, and *light* in my presence.

Go forth today in the joy of my victory. Remember, there are no small victories in the kingdom. Every defeat of the enemy is important in your spiritual journey.

And remember this, my child: my love is unchangeable. Let your love grow toward me and my perfect will.

May Twenty-fourth

Paul replied, "Whether quickly or not, I pray to God that not only
you but also all who are listening to me today might become
such as I am—except for these chains."
—Acts 26:29

This is my word to you today: forget yourself and let your heart go out to others. Seek to put my will ahead of yours, and all will be well.

May Twenty-fifth

I believe that I shall see the goodness of the LORD in the land of the living.
—Psalm 27:13

It is not for you to understand the mysteries of my kingdom, my child. It is for you to enter into them by faith. Your rational, reasoning, questioning mind has put many barriers in your way. You remain "outside" the mystery, looking in—or even looking away—rather than entering through the open door. Remember, child, that I tore the temple veil from top to bottom—that people like you might come into the holy of holies. I want to see you get beyond where you are and taste the goodness of the Lord as you have not done.

May Twenty-sixth

He replied, "It is not for you to know times or periods that the Father
has set by his own authority."
—Acts 1:7

Truly I say to you, my child, it is enough that you hear and receive these simple words of encouragement and assurance. The boundaries of your mind and experience are such that there will always be things too hard for you to understand. Your demand to know must be replaced by a desire to love, to obey, to please me. That is the real path to blessing and fulfillment. The "knowledge path" is never going to fill your deepest needs. Re-think, and be more diligent to find what I have for you.

May Twenty-seventh

Turn now, all of you from your evil way,
and amend your ways and your doings.
—Jeremiah 18:11b

Remember what I have told you, my child: repentance is not regret. It is not remorse over sins remembered. It is *change*. It is a decisive step away from the past into the light of my grace and love. Yes, remorse and regret will remain, for the memory of the break in fellowship with me can serve as an added stimulant to resist temptation when it comes. Foolish one! Do not think that drawing near to me will cause temptation to cease. The trials will come, but there is abundant grace waiting for you each time I call you to go through the valley.

May Twenty-eighth

*If you keep my commandments, you will abide in my love, just as I have
kept my Father's commandments and abide in his love.*
—John 15:10

No child of mine is ordinary. Each one is precious—not the product of mass
production. Of course you must be warned against thinking too highly of yourself, because your tendency is to go from the depths of self-hate and rejection to
the height of self-love and congratulation. My love for you is a steady, unchanging love that is not based on your uniqueness or on your worthiness. It is hard
for you to grasp the reality of it, but my Spirit has brought the reality of it to you.
You can abide in my love because my love is here for you to abide in. I want you
to remember this today. I am here, and I love you.

May Twenty-ninth

There they shall be in great terror, in terror such as has not been.
—Psalm 53:5a

I see in my people too much cowardly fear—that is just another form of self-love. They seek signs and wonders, and miss the real wonders that are taking place before their eyes. This is the blindness of heart that looks and does not see.

There is enough ground for fear in everyone that it is easily exploited by the enemy for his purposes—but he must have the ground of self-love before he can affect his work. I call my people to move forward into a future known to me alone. I repeat—a future known to me alone. Do not try to discern it before its time. Sufficient for today are my blessings and my promises.

May Thirtieth

O LORD, you will ordain peace for us, for indeed,
all that we have done, you have done for us.
—Isaiah 26:12

In my Spirit there is peace. In my Presence there is "an indescribable and glorious joy" (1 Peter 1:8). My throne-room is filled with praise. It is my pleasure to see my children rejoicing in me. This is why, when you enter the secret place of prayer and praise, your heart is touched deeply with this hidden joy. It is a foretaste of that which awaits the faithful soul, and is meant as a bulwark against the evil that assails you in this world.

There is another world—a world that you know now by faith. You are not yet ready for that world, but these glimpses are my gifts to you, that you may abide in my love and fight the good fight to the end. Be at peace, my child. In my spirit there is peace.

May Thirty-first

"I am Alpha and the Omega," says the Lord God, who is, and who was
and who is to come, the Almighty.
—Revelation 1:8

I am the beginning and source of your faith. I am the fount from which flow
the streams of life. I am the truth that banishes the darkness of imagination
and delusion. I am the end and perfection of your journey. Not only the
beginning and ending, my child, but the way between. It is only in me that
you will walk the homeward path. By staying *with* me, living *in* me, you can
finish your course with joy. That is my desire for you—that you finish your
course with joy.

JUNE

This is my Father's world,
And to my listening ears,
All nature sings, and round me
Rings the music of the spheres.

This is my Father's world:
I rest me in the thought
Of rocks and trees, of skies and seas;
His hands the wonder wrought.

This is my Father's world,
The birds their carols raise,
The morning light, the lily white,
Declare their Maker's praise.

This is my Father's world:
He shines in all that's fair;
In the rustling grass I hear him pass,
He speaks to me everywhere.

This is my Father's world,
O let me ne'er forget
That though the wrong seems oft so strong,
God is the Ruler yet.

This is my Father's world:
The battle is not done;
Jesus who died shall be satisfied,
And earth and heaven be one.

—Maltbie D. Babcock, 1858–1901

June First

"Have I been with you all this time, Philip,
and you still do not know me?"
—John 14:9a

Little faith is better than no faith. Little faith in me is better than great faith in yourself. I do not despise your little faith, but I do mean for it to grow. You have been in this way too long to be content with such a small and shriveled faith. I deserve better! I have not asked you for great human strength and courage. I know your frame and your fearful nature. But I have given you plenty of "faith material" with which to grow a robust faith. Where is the harvest, my child? Where?

June Second

For he knows how we were made; he remembers that we are dust.
—Psalm 103:14

"Dust thou art and to dust shalt thou return" (Book of Common Prayer) was spoken only of the physical flesh—the grain of wheat that must fall into the ground. The physical world is passing away and is destined to decay. But my kingdom, my realm, is of another kind. Your glimpses of it are meant to reassure you and yes, lure you away from this passing-away world. Cling not to the world, my child. Let it fall away in my providential plan, and reach forth to grasp the eternal that will never fail. There is no sorrow in the loss if your heart sees and seeks the better part.

June Third

But when he noticed the strong wind, he became frightened, and beginning to sink, he cried out, "Lord, save me!" Jesus immediately reached out his hand and caught him. . . .
—Matthew 14:30–31a

Come nearer to me, my child, and do not be afraid. As I reached out to Peter when his faith failed and he began to sink in the boisterous sea, so I am reaching out to you. You do not have to fear me—for my love is greater than your sin.

You still put too much stock in what others think of you. Their good or bad opinions mean too much to you. So you take too much delight in the one, and suffer too much pain in the other. I am your Shield and great Reward (see Genesis 15:1). I am the Lord who forgives and redeems you. I am he whose love is unchangeable—and I offer you a fellowship deeper and more stable than you have ever known. I can be the crowning experience of your life—if you will come nearer to me, and not be afraid of me.

June Fourth

Heal me, O LORD, and I shall be healed. . . . for you are my praise.
—Jeremiah 17:14

Praise my goodness, my child, in all things. The pain which I allow in your life, as well as the pleasure, is filled with my goodness. By praising my goodness, you extract the sweetness known only to those who love me.

I have called you to be an instrument of praise. Most of my world is still full of bitterness and complaint. My goodness is ignored or rationalized, and people pass away without claiming the hidden blessing. I call forth instruments of praise. These are souls who can hear and *begin* to recognize the truth—a truth so magnificent, so full of grace, that people find it hard to believe.

Praise opens the heart to receive the truth of my goodness. It is not by reasoning, argument, or logic—but by *praise* that this truth will build the temple for my dwelling in your heart. Praise my goodness, my child, in all things.

June Fifth

"I am asking on their behalf; I am not asking on behalf of the world, but on behalf of those who you gave me, because they are yours. All mine are yours, and yours are mine; and I have been glorified in them."
—John 17:9–10

"I am yours." You have said these words many, many times with no real conviction in your heart of what they meant. You are beginning to realize at a new level their awesome truth.

But now, my child, I say to you, "I am yours." This is no one-way relationship; it involves self-giving on both sides. Just as in marriage both must give and receive—so with our relationship. Before you are ready to say with blessed assurance that you are mine, I had *given* myself to you. In very truth, "I am yours."

June Sixth

*. . . to the praise of his glorious grace that he freely bestowed
on us in the Beloved.*
—Ephesians 1:6

My works are mercy. My paths are peace. Your mind is still full of turbulence, because you still long for a false peace. The peace I give is not dependent on the favor or goodwill of others, and you must let go of your demand that they think well of you. For that demand has its own pain and sickness embedded in it.

I call you to my peace—a peace that passes understanding, a peace free from your life-long striving to be accepted by others. Know, my child, that I have accepted you and loved you with an everlasting love. You have not yet accepted my acceptance—and thereby have robbed yourself of much inner rest. Let them rest who hate you. It is not important that others love you. Blessings abound in the path I have chosen for you. My paths are peace, and my works are mercy.

June Seventh

. . . but he said to me, "My grace is sufficient for you, for power is made perfect in weakness."
—2 Corinthians 12:9a

My strength is made perfect in weakness. This is an eternal truth, and you must learn what it means. I am mindful of your weakness, and your life is in my keeping. The days of your life are numbered—known to me alone. You have seen that I am the repairer of ruins, the builder-up of waste places. You do not have to understand why or how this happens. What I call you to do is to rejoice in my works, to see and greet them for what they are.

Greater works are yet to unfold. My blessings are not running out, but they are for those who enter the secret place of my dwelling. Enter with me every day. Guard the sacrifice as Abraham did of old. Be faithful to the end, and I will give you the crown of life.

June Eighth

*. . . as sorrowful, yet always rejoicing; as poor, yet making many rich;
as having nothing, and yet possessing everything.*
—2 Corinthians 6:10

You are never nearer to me than when your heart is overwhelmed with sorrow
and uncertainty. You cannot fathom or understand this reality yet, my child,
but you can accept it. My Spirit is given, not simply to give you times of joy
and brightness, but to guide and lead you through the dark places.

Be of good cheer, and let no clouds keep you from embracing my blessings today, however they may come. Do not hold back from those who reach out
to you. Make an extra effort to show your appreciation to them—for my sake.
As surely as I am God, I will be with you. Count on it, build on it. I am
with you *always*.

June Ninth

The LORD, your God, is in your midst, a warrior who gives victory;
he will rejoice over you with gladness, he will renew you in his love;
he will exult over you with loud singing. . .
—Zephaniah 3:17

My mercy is new every morning in hearts that seek me. You can pray no better prayer than to entreat my mercy on those you love. It is not that I *need* your prayers, my child, but that I allow you to participate in the joy of my goodness through your prayers. Your belief and your prayers *do* make a difference, for I have made a place for them in my plan.

Go now into your day with the full assurance that your prayer has been heard, and my mercy is renewed.

June Tenth

You have kept count of my tossings; put my tears in your bottle.
Are they not in your record?
—Psalm 56:8

You are still a wandering sheep, scurrying about in your mind in various corners of my pasture. You still gaze out over the protective wall I have erected for your safety, and let your mind go after that which I have denied you. This inevitably brings turmoil and confusion when you could be advancing in a tranquil, settled stability. It is natural for lambs and young rams to frolic in playful wandering, but in maturity I expect more—a graver, more serious focus on the eternal verities I have revealed to you in my love. Let my word dwell in you richly as you choose to dwell in my will.

June Eleventh

"For those who want to save their life will lose it, and those who lose their life for my sake, and for the sake of the gospel, will save it."
—Mark 8:35

My child, give over your desire to be liked or loved. You are much too easily affected by signs of being slighted. I have told you that I love you with an everlasting love. My love determines what I allow to come into your life. Yes, my *love* determines that, so be at peace and learn to love others with an undemanding, unself-conscious love, which I will give you—if you seek it sincerely and earnestly.

June Twelfth

"You are worthy, our Lord and God, to receive glory and honor and power, for you created all things, and by your will they existed and were created."
—Revelation 4:11

You are held in the hand that holds the world. You are kept by the power that rules the universe. I have said, "No one will snatch you from my hand" (see John 10:28). It is not your feelings that keep you. It is not even your faith—for I know that grows and lessens quickly under differing circumstances. No, it is my hand that holds you, my child, and protects you when you are least aware of it.

When your eyes are open and you are able to see this reality, give thanks and offer praise. When you cannot see or feel the reality, still give thanks and offer praise. That is an act of faith with which I am pleased. And by the exercise of your faith, this reality will grow stronger and steadier.

June Thirteenth

You ask and do not receive, because you ask wrongly, in order to spend what you get on your pleasures.
—James 4:3

Desires granted, desires denied—both flow from my sovereign will. You see and recognize my goodness in those I have granted. You do not yet see and recognize *clearly* my goodness in those I have denied. But it is all the same—my goodness at work for your good. It could not be otherwise, my child. Even now, as you wait long-delayed answers to your prayers, my work is still going on. Your faith is still weak and unstable. A small setback throws you into confusion. My goal for you far exceeds what you can think or imagine. So do not spend time and energy mourning the loss of desires denied. Let them go in their time and be replaced by hopes that harmonize with my loving will.

June Fourteenth

*And just as I have watched over them to pluck up and break
down, to overthrow, destroy, and bring evil, so I will watch over
them to build and to plant, says the LORD.*
—Jeremiah 31:28

Yes, you need me. I am your life, your breath, and you are sustained every moment by my power and my will. Not a sparrow falls without my permission. The world seems to be out of control. But I have set limits on its freedom, and I keep faithful watch over my own. Yes, "the whole world lies under the power of the evil one" (1 John 5:19b)—through the disobedience and rebellion of my children. The way is still narrow that leads to life, and few there are who find and follow it. Your little world is a small one, but my Spirit within is ever pushing out the borders to make room for my loving concern to live in you. Let this happen. Let pride and prejudice fall away, and see the beauty and joy of allowing my love to reign where your pettiness and self-righteousness ruled and crippled. Yes, my child, you need me. I am your life, and will be your greater life—if you will.

June Fifteenth

"[F]or the LORD does not see as mortals see; they look on the outward appearance, but the LORD looks on the heart."
—I Samuel 16:7b

I know your heart better than you know it. I am acquainted with all its foibles and failings. I know its dark corners and its supreme concentration on itself. Yet I do not despise your cries and groans for greater stability and light. I have come to aid—to save—not to condemn. I am doing a work within, and you have my solemn, sovereign word: I will complete it. All I ask of you is that you continue to be open to me, and follow through in obedience to my word. It shall be well with you, that I may be glorified.

June Sixteenth

You show me the path of life. In your presence there is fullness of joy; in your right hand are pleasures forevermore.
—Psalm 16:11

I am your soul's delight. In my presence there is *fullness* of joy. I give you, my child, a foretaste of heaven's pleasure when your heart floods with joy and thanksgiving. The road before you is purposely obscure. You do not need the burden of knowing the details. Grace abounds in each hard place, and I am with you in all you face. Keep your eyes on the goal—to finish the race and win the crown. The crown is for all who are faithful, not just a few. Keep listening to me. That is important. You still have far to go to maintain a listening attitude. Your mind is still too cluttered with opinions and self-will. This is a training process I have brought you to. Be faithful and the fruit of the process will be good. Delight in me. My goodness is ever before you and never runs out.

June Seventeenth

". . . do not worry beforehand about what you are to say; but say
whatever is given you at that time. . . ."
—Mark 13:11b

I communicate with you, my child, in many different ways. Sometimes a thought is given, full-blown, as it were, and it is yours to act on, to accept or reject. Sometimes my communication is wordless silence—a "sense" of my mercy and love. However it comes, I want you to become more aware and sensitive to the living reality that I am with you and that the "lines" are open. You do not call me in vain, nor speak to an empty space. Remember that, believe it, practice it.

June Eighteenth

While they were talking and discussing, Jesus himself came near and went with them, but their eyes were kept from recognizing him.
—Luke 24:15–16

I will be with you, communicating my word to you throughout this day. Keep your ears and heart open, so that my word will bear the fruitful harvest for which I send it. Walk with me, my child—and learn to be more aware of my presence in your life.

June Nineteenth

But Lot's wife, behind him, looked back, and she became a pillar of salt.
—Genesis 19:26

Move ahead on this path. Do not linger over past memories and failures. They are gone, but if you dwell on them, they will keep you from present obedience. My mercy, not your goodness, is your hope. The time is now for you to reclaim the lost years and enter into the harvest years. Move ahead on this path. Redeem the time—and enjoy it.

Forgive me Father! I have a tendency to dwell on the past and my past sins. Let me focus on today (one day at a time)!

June Twentieth

Jesus straightened up and said to her, "Woman, where are they? Has no one condemned you?" She said, "No one, sir." And Jesus said, "Neither do I condemn you. Go your way, and from now on do not sin again."
—John 8:10–11

Open your heart to receive my word, and open your mouth to speak it. Open your arms to receive and return my love through others. Your way is known, your path is secure. "[N]o evil shall befall you, no scourge come near your tent" (Psalm 91:10).

It is not necessary to dwell in the shame and condemnation that old memories bring up. Let them drive you quickly to me, my child, and let me assure you that my blood cleanses from *all* sin. Leave behind what is behind, and set your face forward to the future I am giving you day by day. Steady your thoughts on me and let go of the shame and condemnation.

June Twenty-first

When you pass through the waters, I will be with you; and through the rivers, they shall not overwhelm you; when you walk through fire you shall not be burned, and the flame shall not consume you. . . . Because you are precious in my sight, and honored, and I love you. . . .
—Isaiah 43:2, 4a

Go peacefully amid the cares of this day. Allow my peace to prevail over anxious or worried thoughts. Remember, my child, that the race is not to the swift, nor the battle to the strong. My way is still a hidden one from the natural eye, and only by faith can you behold the wonder and glory of it. But if you choose, you can behold—and be held in the way.

June Twenty-second

And being found in human form, he humbled himself and became obedient to the point of death——even death on a cross.
—Philippians 2:7b–8

Dear to my heart are those who will follow me in my humiliation. The world can still recognize goodness and self-denial, even though it loves evil and self-assertion. Those who will put down the secret longing to be lifted up in the eyes of others enter into a secret place where I love to abide.

The desire for recognition and appreciation still lives in your heart. I will aid you in mercy as you are willing to receive my aid, in putting this deadly desire to death. It *can* be done——and *will* be done if you are willing. Remember, the desire holds you back from me. What folly, my child, to linger there when I hold out such a prize for you!

June Twenty-third

On the Sabbath day we went outside the gate by the river, where we
supposed there was a place of prayer. . . .
—Acts 16:13a

My dear child, I am nearer than you think, more present to your mind and
heart than you know. Your longings for unity and harmony are the fruit of
my implanting. Let them encourage you to reach out in prayer for others,
for prayers do make a difference. The world could be very different if my
people had learned to pray. Your world and the world of those you love will
be affected by your faithfulness or lack of faithfulness in prayer. The yearning
you feel for "connectedness" is but a drawing of my Spirit toward the unity of
spirit and harmony of heart that I will for my people. The place of prayer is
a trysting place of the Spirit.

June Twenty-fourth

[Do] not forget the works of God, but keep his commandments; and they should not be like their ancestors, a stubborn and rebellious generation, a generation whose heart was not steadfast. . . .
—Psalm 78:7b–8a

Like trees planted by rivers of water, I plant the souls of my children in the deep soil of my love. Like trees planted in good soil I look for fruit, 'the product of life lived unto me. Sink your roots deep into my love and bear good fruit.

June Twenty-fifth

The LORD is king! Let the earth rejoice. . . .
—Psalm 97:1a

I have heard your prayers and the longing of your heart. I will not leave you nor forsake you, my child. The road ahead is clear and you have nothing to fear. Rejoice with me in the way. The songs I have given my people are songs of rejoicing. They are more than a stirring of the emotions. They are the sounds of triumph over the enemy of your soul. Use them as weapons in the fight.

Be at peace with your neighbor—do not allow opinions to wound and separate you from one another. Be careful to fight on the right front, and do not be tricked into trying to win your point. This is important.

* Be careful to fight on the right front, and do not be tricked into trying to win your point. This is important.

2017

June Twenty-sixth

"Everyone who belongs to the truth listens to my voice."
—John 18:37c

The quiet impressions that I bring to your mind are to be heeded and treasured. Do not wait for some overwhelming word, but learn to listen attentively to the still, small voice. I will protect and guard you from being led in wrong paths—only be courageous and dare to listen, hear, and heed!

June Twenty-seventh

You desire truth in the inward being; therefore teach me
wisdom in my secret heart.
—Psalm 51:6

Do not fret yourself over the unfinished state of those you love. Trust me
that I am still at work and can make all things new. Truly I say to you, look
up, wait, pray, and believe, and you will see my glory. I am the true and
faithful One, and my promises *never* fail.

God is not finished with me
and my family yet!

June Twenty-eighth

Create in me a clean heart, O God, and put a new and right spirit within me. Do not cast me away from your presence, and do not take your holy spirit from me. Restore to me the joy of your salvation, and sustain in me a willing spirit.
—Psalm 51:10–12

It is enough that you wait for my word and continue to draw your mind away from its wanderings. I remember who and whose you are. And my mercy covers your feeble efforts. There are no spiritual heroics here—just your needy, broken spirit and my all-sufficient Spirit of grace. I do not want you to become discouraged at what seems a lack of progress in these morning meetings. Yours is not an unusual case. Persevere, my child, persevere.

June Twenty-ninth

"Peace I leave with you; my peace I give to you. I do not give to you as the world gives. Do not let your hearts be troubled, and do not let them be afraid."
—John 14:27

I want my word to reach many hearts. My fatherly care extends to all my children, and many of them do not know me. They are in need of truth and light. The entrance of my word gives light—so I send it into dark places. All I require of you is a willingness to be a channel of truth and hope. It is a simple ministry, and it is life-bringing to those who sit in the shadow of death. If you will keep this in mind, we can accomplish my will. Your blessings will be multiplied, and your reward will be more than you can know. So you have nothing to lose by your willingness to be a fool for my sake.

I want to be a fool for Jesus!

June Thirtieth

"*The time is fulfilled, and the kingdom of God has come near;
repent, and believe in the good news.*"
—Mark 1:15

It is my pleasure to give good gifts to my children. I do not give according to their deserving, but as I see best. Sometimes I withhold gifts, because they would not bring a blessing with them. Material gifts are a special problem in this regard. They are easily turned into distractions and misuse. So I withhold them, waiting until the soul is ready and able to bear them. When the heart attaches itself to worldly goods, the blessing is lost. Walk carefully now, my child, amid the countless gifts I have given you. Don't let the gifts come between us.

Father,
   Please don't let my many
blessings come between us!

JULY

From every stormy wind that blows,
    From every swelling tide of woes,
There is a calm, a sure retreat:
    'Tis found beneath the mercy seat.

There is a scene where spirits blend,
    Where friend holds fellowship with friend;
And heaven comes down our souls to greet
    And glory crowns the mercy seat.

Talk with us, Lord, Thyself reveal,
    While here o'er earth we rove;
Speak to our hearts, and let us feel
    The kindling of Thy love.

Here then, my God, vouchsafe to stay,
    And bid my heart rejoice;
My bounding heart shall own Thy sway,
    And echo to Thy voice.

Thou callest me to seek Thy face,
    'Tis all I wish to seek;
To hear the whispers of Thy grace,
    And hear Thee inly speak.

—Hugh Stowell, 1799–1865

July First

My dear child, be content with my love. I see your heart still searching for others to love and respect you. Each time you go on such a search you are seeking vanity—emptiness. Do you not know that yet?

It grieves my heart to see my children, to whom I have revealed my mercy and lovingkindness so powerfully and clearly, still go "whoring" after emptiness. And so I ask you again, my child, be *content* with my love. It is enough, and you will come to see that it is more than you can ask or think. But it is seen and felt in its fullness only when you abandon the useless search for that which can never satisfy.

July Second

They shall ask the way to Zion with faces turned toward it,
and they shall come and join themselves to the LORD by an
everlasting covenant that will never be forgotten.
—Jeremiah 50:5

My glory is seen in the mundane—the ordinary paths of the day. Look for me more faithfully, my child, and you will surely meet me there. Hidden from your eyes, I watch over you. Unseen, I protect and provide manifold blessings. Unthanked, I still provide.

You would be greatly blessed if you would cultivate and *practice* my presence more faithfully. My presence is there—*with* you. Did I not promise? "And remember, I am with you always, to the end of the age" (Matthew 28:20). That was not spoken just to the disciples on the Mount where I left them. It was my word to my people—those who come to me and follow me in their hearts. It is for you, my child, it is for you! How weak and foolish you are not to let me be your constant companion!

My glory *can* be seen in the ordinary paths. Will you look more faithfully?

July Third

. . . just as he chose us in Christ before the foundation of the world to be holy and blameless before him in love.
—Ephesians 1:4

My dear child, I speak to you in love. Your fear of what I might say grows out of an old, sick, and distorted view of me and my relation to my children. You never ceased to love your own children, and you had no desire that their fear of you would remain in that relationship. In the same way, "the fear of the LORD is the *beginning* of wisdom" (Proverbs 9:10), and "perfect love casts out fear" (1 John 4:18a). That means that as you mature, your only fear is that of offending or grieving my love—not the self-oriented fear of what I might *do* to you.

I speak to you in love because that is the essence of our relationship, from my perspective. I know that you still have far to go, but I do not despise you nor condemn you for it. Keep growing!

July Fourth

For I the LORD do not change, therefore you,
O children of Jacob, have not perished.
—Malachi 3:6

I am with you today, my child, and you have nothing to fear. Go forth in the joy and anticipation of my blessing. Put aside needless worries and thoughts of what might be. They only tangle and crowd the path laid out before you. Be confident and of good courage, for the cause is mine, not yours. I will keep my promises. There is no variableness or changing in me. You shall yet see my hand at work to bring about my design and desire—so be prepared. Faith is the necessary key to unlock the treasury I have in store. I will help your unbelief if you will stay close to me in your need.

July Fifth

Incline your ear, and come to me; listen, so that you may live.
I will make with you an everlasting covenant,
my steadfast, sure love for David.
—Isaiah 55:3

Call upon me and I will answer you. I have said this to you many times. It is enough that I have said it. You can build on that simple word. Call on me, and I will answer you. No one ever called on me in vain.

Do not fear to come to me in any condition. Do not let your sin deter your coming. I wait to be merciful. I am the Lord who forgives and heals. Do you not know that I know the condition in which you turn to me? I read the thoughts and intentions of the heart. So do not be afraid of offending me. Your separation from me is more harmful than any sin you bring with repentance. Your safety is in staying close to me.

July Sixth

Let us therefore approach the throne of grace with boldness, so that we may receive mercy and find grace to help in time of need.
—Hebrews 4:16

Beside the still waters I bid you pause and rest. Soul-rest needs quietness—the stillness of my presence. Turbulence abounds when you seek your will, when you linger in old guilts and regrets, when you worry about your future or the future of your loved ones. But if you will linger here, my child, and accept the quietness of spirit I offer you, you may go on your way rejoicing in hope. Frantic striving does not accomplish my perfect will, no matter how well-intentioned. "Those who bring thanksgiving as their sacrifice honor me" (Psalm 50:23). So pause, praise, refresh your soul in my still waters, and be renewed.

July Seventh

For, being ignorant of the righteousness that comes from God, and seeking to establish their own, they have not submitted to God's righteousness.
—Romans 10:3

This is my word for you today, my child: put away falsehood and live in reality. Let go of the vain imaginations that invade your thoughts with distracting frequency. Forge a weapon of prayer against these energy-draining intruders. Learn to recognize the tricks of your adversary.

My presence is with you, though you do not sense or realize it. It is not a palpable sensation to be sought but a reality to be recognized. I am fulfilling my promises and proceeding with my purpose. You do not need to be babied at this point, but to keep your mind and heart fixed on accomplishing my will for you.

July Eighth

"Whenever you stand praying, forgive, if you have anything against any-one; so that your Father in heaven may also forgive you your trespasses."
—Mark 11:25

And now, my child, be at peace with yourself and with others. Let no grudge or hurt remain lodged in your heart. Remember my words, "Forgive us our debts, as we also have forgiven our debtors," and struggle against the desire to hold on to some injury from the past.

A free people is a forgiven people. A free soul is a forgiving soul. Where you hold back forgiveness you keep yourself in bondage. There is much to learn about this miracle—the grace of forgiveness. And there is much need of it, both in your life and in the life of others. Don't wait for them, but heed my word for yourself.

July Ninth

". . . I am with you always, to the end of the age."
—Matthew 28:20b

These things I have spoken to you to bring to your remembrance the basic realities of your life. At the center of all that comes to you, I am present—by will or by allowance—but you are never, *never* without me. If you could grasp this with surety, how great a difference it could make in your experience. When I said to my disciples, "I am with you always, to the end of the age," I included you—your specific time and need—in that promise. This is the central, basic reality that can drive away the demons and shadows of the night.

July Tenth

*They heard the sound of the LORD God walking in the garden at the time
of the evening breeze, and the man and his wife hid themselves from the
presence of the LORD God among the trees of the garden.*
—Genesis 3:8

Again I tell you, I am the Lord who heals you. My promises are still in effect.
I see your emotions vacillate between hope and despair. Your fear is your
enemy. Remember, my child, "perfect love casts out fear" (1 John 4:18b).
There is *no* fear in love. I have not forgotten to be gracious. My heart is open
to you. Your fear closes your heart to me. You shall yet see the wonder of my
grace. I have promised, and I will be faithful. I have spoken, and I will per-
form. It is not up to you to bring it about. This is my concern. Only believe!
Only trust! Only confess your fear and flee to the Rock!

July Eleventh

Look to him, and be radiant; so your faces shall never be ashamed.
—Psalm 34:5

My child, do not hurry. Wait for me. Let the natural impatience of your soul be put to death by my delay. I know your need. You need not distress yourself. I always come on time. You will learn this truth if you will continue to wait on me. I come laden with the gifts you need. Before you call, I am prepared with my answer. Yet your call is necessary, because you need to become needy in your own eyes.

Take your eyes off the circumstances that cause inner turmoil. Leave them to me. Let my Spirit convict and convert your heart—not out of fear of what others may think or say or do—but in holy sorrow and compunction of heart toward me. You have yet much to learn about true conviction, deep repentance, and the peace that forgiveness brings.

July Twelfth

Your proud heart has deceived you. . . .
—Obadiah 3a

I the Lord your God am speaking to you. Heaven and earth shall pass away—but my love is eternal. My child, you still have far to go and much to receive before the fullness of this truth is in you. You still operate on the basis of merit and punishment—of being good and being bad. You still take pride in the works of my grace, and do not pay the fullness of tribute to me. The momentary lift you get from such pride comes with a high price. It damages your soul and delays your progress toward maturity. Learn to recognize these feelings and quickly bring them to me before great damage is done, and you find yourself in enemy territory. It can be done. It is not without hope of change, even though your nature is badly bent in this pattern. Credit and glory are not the true fulfillment you have thought them to be. They are chains that bind you to a changing, dying, fickle world. But you *can* break the chains!

July Thirteenth

So let us not grow weary in doing what is right, for we will reap at the harvest time, if we do not give up.
—Galatians 6:9

My dear child, wait awhile. Do not be impatient when you do not see an immediate answer to your prayers. Waiting is an important part of the prayer process. It is a great separator of the trivial from the heartfelt request. It is a time for refining your motives in asking. It is an *active* time, not merely an unwanted delay.

Wait awhile. My ears are open to your needs and the needs of those you hold before me. No prayer is wasted. In my love, I take them into account and turn them to good effect, even when the answer is not what you hoped or wanted. Knowing that secret, continue to pray—and wait awhile. You will have ample cause to rejoice.

July Fourteenth

He did this to show his righteousness, because in his divine forbearance he
had passed over the sins previously committed; it was to prove
at the present time that he himself is righteous and that he
justifies the one who has faith in Jesus.
—Romans 3:25b–26

It is enough, my child, that you seek to love and obey according to the light I give you, not yours, to unravel the mysteries of life. Be careful not to become hard and withdrawn when you are in the company of those whose thoughts and understandings differ from yours. Seek a quiet and peaceful spirit. In that you will be a blessing instead of a stumbling block. I will be with you to warn when danger approaches. Listen, heed, and obey—and reap the blessing.

July Fifteenth

Come now, let us argue it out, says the Lord: *though your sins
are like scarlet, they shall be like snow. . . .*
—Isaiah 1:18a

Whiter than snow! That is the miracle of the forgiven soul. That is the
miracle of my grace. I seek the sullied and soiled souls of my children,
and I wait to be gracious. I see the turmoil and pain, and I wait to bestow
the balm of Gilead. I am afflicted in the afflictions of my children, but
there is no cheap shortcut to alleviate their pain. I am God and not man.
My universe moves according to my design and wisdom, and I uphold it
according to my wisdom and power.

Yet I am moved to bring healing for hurts, and salvation for sinners.
My love reaches out, stirs and troubles the wayward heart, that it might turn
and live.

Whiter than snow! That is the miracle I desire to make possible by my
grace.

July Sixteenth

"How long will you go limping with two different opinions?
If the LORD is God, follow him."
—I Kings 18:21b

Choose this day whom you will serve. Remember, the choice is always yours. The choice is "whom you will serve," not "will you serve?" For if you allow yourself the luxury of thinking you don't need to choose, you have already made a choice.

Do not be foolish, my child, and do not waste the time I am giving you to bring forth a fruitful harvest. The hour is already late, so you need to bear that in mind as you make your choice today.

July Seventeenth

"... [Y]et, not what I want but as you want."
—Matthew 26:39c

You are being tested on many fronts in the circumstances of your life. Each day I offer you a way through these perplexities and give you the privilege of making good choices. This is my grace at work. You are not a robot, programmed to behave in a certain way. I have created and redeemed you to give you this inestimable privilege. Keep alert to what I am saying, my child, so that with the test you will also see and choose my way through. Set negative feelings aside and press on toward the goal.

July Eighteenth

Surely goodness and mercy shall follow me all the days of my life, and I shall dwell in the house of the LORD my whole life long.
—Psalm 23:6

It is time again to cast all your cares and burdens on me. There is a way to carry your responsibilities lightly but not carelessly. It is found here at my mercy seat, my throne of grace. If you will bring these cares and burdens to me and *trust me* to help you, you can go out in peace and carry out your part. That is my plan and my wish for you and all my loved ones. It is not a passive, presumptuous attitude I am asking of you, but a loving, trusting expectancy that grace will abound and the way will appear. Faith is walking and working in this expectancy.

July Nineteenth

But rejoice insofar as you are sharing Christ's sufferings, so that you
may also be glad and shout for joy when his glory is revealed. If you are
reviled for the name of Christ, you are blessed, because the spirit of glory,
which is the Spirit of God, is resting on you.
—1 Peter 4:13–14

Not in the height of elation is true joy to be found, my child, but in the
quiet places of the heart. Too much "happiness" tends to make you giddy and
unwise. A more somber scene is safer for you.

Yet I know your longing for "indescribable and glorious joy" (1 Peter
1:8b). I know how hard it is for you to allow gladness to drive away shadows
of doubt and fear. So I bid you, child, to draw near to my heart. Do not
worry about details of feelings, and avoid introspection about your motives.
I will attend to all that. I want you to be a child of the upward look. I want
you to seek my face, my merciful appearance in all the circumstances of
your day. This will take concentration and focus—because it is so new to
you. But *do* try!

July Twentieth

Then he said, "Come no closer! Remove the sandals from your feet, for the place on which you are standing is holy ground."
—Exodus 3:5

In the midst of trouble and uncertainty, I am still your peace. This is the peace that passes all understanding, because it is not tied to, nor is it dependent on, the pleasantness of the circumstances of your life. I know the situation you face. I am still Lord of it. What I ask of you is to draw near to me and stay near to me until this storm has passed. Have I not promised to be with you in trouble? Is my arm shortened that it cannot save? Turn from the fear and unbelief that arise in your heart at the first sign of trouble. Call upon me, and I will answer you. Learn, learn, learn to trust me—and go forward with me. Today's Scripture is not there by accident or "coincidence." "Remove the sandals from your feet, for the place on which you are standing is holy ground." That means the foundation on which you stand in me is holy ground. Believe it and do not fear!

July Twenty-first

Great peace have those who love your law;
nothing can make them stumble.
—Psalm 119:165

It is good to wait in my presence. You are being blessed and fed by my Spirit, even when you hear no words. It is good to keep trusting when your prayers are delayed. You have been long in coming to this place, and there is still much ground to reclaim. You have built a fortress around your mind, and trusted in your own thoughts and opinions rather than in me. Your thoughts failed you when great need arose, and you were faced with their inability to help. I have not failed you, but you forfeited much peace by your choices. It is good to wait in my presence. This, too, is part of my work to help you regain and reclaim lost ground.

July Twenty-second

*Honor and majesty are before him; strength
and beauty are in his sanctuary.*
—Psalm 96:6

The riches of my Word are hidden from the natural eye that sees the outer "shell" and may even admire what it sees. But to those who are willing to ask, to seek, and to knock, my treasury unlocks its greater beauty. Here the soul feasts, and here it finds joys that it cannot describe. Truly, my child, those who find these riches can say, "The boundary lines have fallen for me in pleasant places. I have a goodly heritage" (Psalm 16:6). The beauty of holiness is seen and experienced in the garden of love. The glimpses you are given of my beauty and glory are gifts to help you through your hard times. Treasure them and do not forget them.

July Twenty-third

May those who sow in tears reap with shouts of joy.
—Psalm 126:5

The early rain and the latter rain—tears given to water the dry ground of your soul. The early rains were the tears that came in your youth, though you were embarrassed by them and did not understand what they were about. But they opened the ground of your soul to receive impressions of my Spirit and allowed the seed of my word to grow silently within you. The latter rain is your present gift, again to enable your soul to receive my life-giving word. Do not despise the tears, and do not try to delve into secrets hidden from you. Let my word grow to bring forth an abundant harvest.

July Twenty-fourth

"Listen! I am standing at the door, knocking; if you hear my voice and open the door, I will come in to you and eat with you, and you with me."
—Revelation 3:20

My dear child, why is it so hard for you to accept my words of love? Or the reality of my love for you? Have I not proven over and over that I love you with a supernatural and unfailing love? Has my care ever been lacking? Yet you draw back, frightened, guilty, defensive—against me.

I will not force myself beyond that inner citadel. I am standing at the door, knocking—for my nature is to respect what I have created and given life to. When I said, "I will come in to you and eat with you," I meant that a whole world of friendship awaits those who hear my voice and allow me entrance to the inmost recesses. It is Love that stands—that pleads. Let me take full charge. Don't let pride, fear, jealousy, or any shame keep you from love's goal. My dear child, why do you think I died for you?

July Twenty-fifth

. . . the blood of Jesus his Son cleanses us from all sin.
—I John I:7b

The wounds of the soul must be cleansed before healing can take place. The cleansing process is painful for you, because the stains are the result of your sinful choices in the past. The more you are aware of this, the easier it makes your cooperation with the process. The light of truth exposes the ugliness of these sores, but the balm of Gilead then restores lost beauty. Marvel at the goodness that directs my operation, and do not flinch at the necessary pain.

July Twenty-sixth

For we do not have a high priest who is unable to sympathize
with our weaknesses, but we have one who in every respect
has been tested as we are, yet without sin.
—Hebrews 4:15

Hidden in the mystery of my love are all the events of your life, good and bad. Have I not said, "As far as the east is from the west, so far have I removed your transgression from me" (see Psalm 103:12)? This is not an empty phrase. It is a proclamation of divine mercy to helpless sinners. Forgiveness is the key that unlocks my fulfillment—forgiving those who have wronged or hurt you and *accepting* forgiveness for the wrongs you have committed.

My dear Son entered into the darkest valley of suffering to change the power of guilt into the power of forgiveness. My people know little—almost nothing—of what he accomplished there. Enter into this truth as you have never done and invite others to venture in. In doing so, you enter further into my heart.

July Twenty-seventh

. . . for the Spirit searches everything, even the depths of God.
—I Corinthians 2:10b

In your dreams I have spoken, and in dark language I have communicated with your spirit. You do not have to understand with your rational mind all that I am doing. You need only to be obedient to that which I clearly speak.

There are depths in the human heart that can only be plumbed by my Spirit. The heart is a deep cavern, and there are many hiding places where sin lurks undetected. The confusions you feel come from these smelly places, and the Spirit seeks them out as you cease resisting him. "Truth in the inward being" (Psalm 51:6a) comes by the Spirit of truth occupying and enlightening those hidden places.

July Twenty-eighth

. . . and after the earthquake a fire; but the LORD was not in the fire; and
after the fire a sound of sheer silence.
—1 Kings 19:12

I the Lord your God am with you, my child. Walk this day with me, consciously seeking to hear and heed the "sound of sheer silence" of my Spirit within your heart. I will speak to you and guide you. Only be careful to listen!

You cannot know the way or the path to follow on your own. Confusion is sown by the adversary to trap the unwary. But I have promised, and my promise is faithful; I will show the path through the maze.

Your faith will be strengthened if you will be careful to heed my words. You will grow more confident in this new walk, and that is good. I want your faith to become more simple and ready to act. Are you sufficient for this? No, but remember, my child, your sufficiency will be in *me*. And there is no lack there!

July Twenty-ninth

Your word is a lamp to my feet and a light to my path. I have sworn an oath and confirmed it, to observe your righteous ordinances.
—Psalm 119:105–106

It is my pleasure to give good gifts to my children—and the gift of my word is my choicest gift. You must learn to treasure it more deeply, my child, for it is not to be despised. Grieve not my Spirit by taking a casual attitude toward the gift I am giving you.

Truly I say to you, do not think the journey is over and the day is done. Do not seek to be released from my yoke and burden. At the right time, you may lay it down, but not before. I will provide the necessary strength and health. Make no mistake about that. Redeem these days—they are harvest days.

July Thirtieth

Open your mouth wide and I will fill it.
—Psalm 81:10b

Write this: I have long put my word in your mouth. You have not known, indeed you cannot know, the purpose and object to which I sent it. It is not your word—it is mine. Be faithful in speaking what I give you. The glory shall not be yours, but mine. Multiply the occasions to praise me by being faithful in what I set before you. Faithfulness brings forth praise.

July Thirty-first

*"For if you forgive others their trespasses, your heavenly Father
will also forgive you; but if you do not forgive others,
neither will your Father forgive your trespasses."*
—Matthew 6:14–15

See how great a fire a little word kindles! See how great a storm surges when one contrary breeze blows! Such is your vanity, my child, that you allow small things to be magnified and treated as great matters. You rob yourself of peace and grieve my Spirit by your persistence in this old pattern.

Do you love me more than these? Do you *want* my presence more than the cheap toys you feel you have lost? Wake up, child! You cannot play with your slights and jealousies and ready yourself for the life beyond. Your words to others must first apply to yourself. Get your heart into harmony with mine. What else matters?

AUGUST

All the way my Savior leads me,
   What have I to ask beside?
Can I doubt His tender mercies,
   Who through life has been my guide?
Heavenly peace, divinest comfort,
   Here by faith in Him to dwell,
For I know whate'er befall me,
   Jesus doeth all things well.
All the way my Savior leads me,
   Cheers each winding path I tread,
Gives me grace for every trial,
   Feeds me with the living bread,
Though my weary steps may falter,
   And my soul athirst may be,
Gushing from the Rock before me,
   Lo! a spring of joy I see.

All the way my Savior leads me;
   Oh, the fullness of His love!
Perfect rest to me is promised
   In my Father's house above.
When my spirit, clothed immortal,
   Wings its flight to realms of day,
This my song through endless ages:
   Jesus led me all the way.

—Fanny J. Crosby, 1820–1915

August First

"Come to me, all you that are weary and are carrying heavy
burdens, and I will give you rest."
—Matthew 11:28

I am your Father and your Savior. There is no reason to be cut off from me. I have called you, and I will sustain you to the end. O you of little faith! How many times have I revealed my tender mercies to you—and yet you fear! Be done with living in the shadows when my light is shining for you. I tell you again: life is to be *lived,* not simply endured. Do not be afraid to reach out, to share your life with others, to extend my blessing to them. I will show you and direct you as you obey. Only *do* live, my child, and learn to trust.

August Second

*Jesus answered them, "Have faith in God. . . . [W]hatever you ask
for in prayer, believe that you have received it, and it will
be yours. Whenever you stand praying, forgive. . . ."*
—Mark 11:22, 24–25a

There are no restrictions to limit the extent of your faith in me. I have not
set bounds on what I am able to do in response to the prayer of faith. The
limits you put on it are your own, and they do limit the extent and outreach
of your prayers. That is a spiritual law which operates for every child of
mine.

Just as muscles atrophy or grow with disuse or use, so faith dwindles or
grows with exercise. I seek vigorous, faith-filled children who, like Gideon,
in spite of fear, went ahead and dared to trust me. Your fear restricts, while
faith releases. It is a barrier to be overcome if you are to move in the glorious
liberty of the children of God. Why wait?

August Third

. . . encouraging one another, and all the more
as you see the Day approaching.
—Hebrews 10:25b

In the early morning light, there is hope for greater light. Shadows flee before the rising sun. Even so, my child, the glimmers of your "early morning light" hold the promise of a clearer day. Shadows of doubt and fear, guilt and sin, cannot stand before my light. I am your light and your promise that hope will not be disappointed. You have light enough for every step of today's journey. Rejoice in it, be thankful for it, and you will see that I *am* the Way, the Truth, and the Life.

August Fourth

From now on there is reserved for me the crown of righteousness,
which the Lord, the righteous judge, will give me on that day, and not
only to me but also to all who have longed for his appearing.
—2 Timothy 4:8

Crowns and honors are mine to give. They are never to be sought for their own sake. My glory is seen in those who do not seek their own. They are blessed with the secret joy that I impart to the humble. Seek humility, my child, as a treasure more precious than gold. Do not despise the humiliations I send or allow, for they are sharp instruments to prune away the rank overgrowth of pride. Look about you and see the signs that I am at work on your proud nature, to make humility a possibility for you. That is a token of my love.

August Fifth

For the wicked shall be cut off, but those who wait for
the LORD shall inherit the land.
—Psalm 37:9

Blessed are those who wait for me. My coming is always on time, but to you it may seem too long delayed. In the waiting, your desire is tested. I have told you to ask, seek, and knock—to keep on asking, seeking, knocking—for in that process a sorting out is taking place, and the depth of your desire is seen. Distractions offer relief from waiting, so beware of the subtlety of their appeal. Fight to stay in focus. I have not abandoned you, and my purpose is still for your good. Remember that always—always, my child. My love for you is an everlasting, eternal love.

August Sixth

*He turns a desert into pools of water, and
parched land into springs of water.*
—Psalm 107:35

My way is in the desert, my child, where hidden springs flow and unexpected oases appear. The desert is the dryness and separateness you feel. You lose sight of the path, you lose sight of the goal of your journey, and you lose sight of the meaning of your days. My oases appear and you are again refreshed, but you cannot stay in that pleasant resting place. My way is in the desert and through the desert—toward your true destination and home. Trudge on, but do not forget your Companion on the way. The journey is not over. The end is not yet.

August Seventh

*The crash of your thunder was in the whirlwind; your lightnings
lit up the world; the earth trembled and shook.*
—Psalm 77:18

My thoughts come to you in the midst of your thoughts. Because you are
still bound by your old habits, you do not recognize or greet them. I still
choose to speak in the "still, small voice" rather than the thunder. My yoke
is easy. I am gentle and lowly of heart. But because I love you and care for
your welfare, I *will* speak in thunder if necessary. So tune your heart to hear.
Be assured that the voice is there, and that it *is* possible to commune with
me more consistently than you have ever known.

August Eighth

. . . again I will say, Rejoice.
—Philippians 4:4b

Rejoice, my child, rejoice. Let praise fill your heart and overflow from your life. Believe in the efficacy of prayers—even your own feeble ones. My ear is open even to the sighs of my children. While you wait to see the changes prayer can bring about, rejoice in faith and drive away the scavengers of doubt that would take away your sacrifice of praise. Praise and faith strengthen and nourish one another. That is why Paul says, "With thanksgiving let your requests be made known to God" (Philippians 4:6b).

August Ninth

Look to him, and be radiant; so your faces shall never be ashamed.
—Psalm 34:5

Lift up your hands and your heart to me and expect my word to be fulfilled. The great sin and barrier to your prayers is your lack of expectant faith. You entertain doubts and accusing thoughts without realizing their true nature and the danger they pose to your welfare. I bid you to believe, but I will not force you to believe. That I have reserved for you. It is a choice, and if you will make it against your fearful thoughts and feelings, you will see its fruit. Leave the hard questions aside, and come as a little child to me.

August Tenth

. . . I am the one who searches minds and hearts. . . .
—Revelation 2:23b

Your days are based on anxiety and fear. These in turn are rooted in pride, fear of looking bad to others. My days bring peace. My timetable is always sufficient to accomplish what I require. Let my peace stand guard over your mind, and let your anxious thoughts fade away like the morning dew. "Oh, how foolish you are, and how slow of heart to believe" (Luke 24:25)! Have I not always been faithful? Give over the reins, my child, give them over that peace may prevail.

August Eleventh

. . . so great a cloud of witnesses. . . .
—Hebrews 12:1a

My dear child, my mercy seat is always open to you. Here you are surrounded by many who have frequented it before you. You are not aware of their presence or their aid in your journey, but they are partners with you in the struggle you face.

Do not be afraid to embrace new understandings as you journey with me. New scenes and new occasions have their place in your growth. You are reluctant to give up old ideas and habits, even as you try new ones. You still fear what others will think about you. But remember how steady my mercy has been, and do not fear to widen the scope of your spiritual vision—it is safe here at the mercy seat.

August Twelfth

"Blessed are the merciful, for they will receive mercy."
—Matthew 5:7

I have this against you, my child, that you show so little mercy to those who need it most. Mercy is not softness nor compromise with truth, but truth without mercy can be hard and sharp. It can build walls when bridges are needed.

As I rehearse the many examples and instances of my mercy to you, remember the parable of the servant who would not forgive the debt of his fellow servant. Learn from this, that I intend my mercy to be multiplied through you to others. Do not be deceived nor think of yourself more highly than you ought to think. While there is yet time, ask for guidance and set your heart to learn and practice being a mercy-giver.

August Thirteenth

. . . who forgives all your iniquity, who heals all thy diseases. . . .
—Psalm 103:3

My child, I am still healing old wounds in your soul. The process is slow and often hidden from your view. But I tell you, for sure, it is taking place. You are not marking time and your circumstances are not accidents. So lift up your head and your heart, and receive each day as a gift. You do not know the end, but I do, and I am leading you toward my goal for you.

August Fourteenth

Even though I walk through the darkest valley, I fear no evil;
for you are with me. . . .
—Psalm 23:4a

My dear child, I have no delight in the suffering of my people. I allow it only for their eternal good. Blessed are those who turn to me in their trouble, for I am a God of mercy and compassion. The valleys through which I call you to go need not frighten you. The shadows and darkness are only for a time. Let your faith grow strong when darkness comes. Faith will overcome where daylight cannot prevail. Suffering purges away the rampant growth of self—if you let it do its work. There are two ways in which I turn it to good: by its pruning and by my healing. In both ways I bring blessing to my chosen ones.

August Fifteenth

For the LORD God is a sun and shield; he bestows favor and honor.
No good thing does the LORD withhold from those who walk uprightly.
—Psalm 84:11

No good thing have I withheld from you, my child. In my wisdom and mercy, I have not allowed you to have many things you wanted, but their denial was a blessing, not a curse. I have showered my gifts on you—in part, because of the frailty and difficulty of your nature. The abundance of my mercy toward you is better than the abundance you could have gathered with a more attractive and winsome nature. The brokenness you have carried inside is a necessary part of this gift, so that it may yet bear the fruit and harvest I intend for it. In the meantime, let it all work its work in your soul and give thanks!

August Sixteenth

Your righteousness is like the mighty mountains, your
judgments are like the great deep. . . .
—Psalm 36:6a

You cannot know the depths of my love as long as you cling to your old life. There are many overt and subtle ways of clinging. You hate to give up the little comforts and satisfactions, fleeting though they are. But they exact a price all out of proportion to their reward. You must become more aware of their temptation, for you too easily give in without a thought of their real and destructive nature. Your mind is a minefield. Your thoughts are weapons in the hand of the adversary, and you do not even recognize them as such. I do not want you to become super-spiritual and unnatural. I do not call you to weirdness. Rather to awareness—full consciousness of the reality of the warfare that is in your life. If you will choose this, I will help you. If you refuse it, you will suffer great loss.

August Seventeenth

On the last day of the festival, the great day, while Jesus was standing there, he cried out, "Let anyone who is thirsty come to me, and let the one who believes in me drink. As the scripture has said, 'Out of the believer's heart shall flow rivers of living water.'"
—John 7:37-38

Draw near to me, my child, and I will not fail to draw near to you. You never seek me in vain, no matter what your feelings tell you. I, the Lord, change not. My face is ever toward you for good, even when you are least aware of it.

Out of the wells of salvation comes the water of life. Drink deeply of this life-giving Spirit, my child, that you may be a conveyor of that water to others. Look for opportunities to witness to my goodness to others, and deny the negative spirit.

Psalm 34:19-20 — "The righteous person may have many troubles, but the Lord delivers him from them all; he protects all his bones, not one of them will be broken."

I had a car accident today — aug. 17, 2017 — God protected me and the young man in the car that I hit from serious injury or broken bones. (South Lake Tahoe)

August Eighteenth

. . . [Y]ou have set my feet in a broad place.
—Psalm 31:8b

A certain man lived in a large, beautiful mansion. It was made of stone and was built to last indefinitely. The house was occupied by a suitable staff of servants, ready to supply his every need. From time to time people would pass by and comment on the beauty and stability of the house, and would wonder what it was like inside. One thing they noticed: a small, rather unsightly path made its way across the lawn to a back servants' entrance. And the man, the owner, always approached his home via this path and through this door. What others did not know was that the man, the owner of this large, beautiful stone mansion, lived in one small servant's room in the back of the house. It had been so long since he even visited the other rooms that he couldn't remember what they looked like, and felt no sense of identity as their owner. Nor did he call on his servants to help him. Instead, he went in and out, afraid of losing his little servant's room, and angry that he found life so dull and uninteresting. He was very conscious of his aches and pains, his changing moods, and often retired to his room hurt and angry at what others said or thought.

Let those hear who have ears to hear. . . .

August Nineteenth

"Come, let us go up to the mountain of the LORD,
to the house of the God of Jacob; that he may teach us his
ways and that we may walk in his paths."
—Isaiah 2:3b

O foolish child! To wonder how I can speak to you and to many others at the same time! Am I not God? Did I not create this world, this universe, by the word of my power? How little you know and understand. Your demand that you understand is a block in your spiritual growth. Faith, believing, trusting—these are far more important than understanding. Understanding will come as the dawn—but it is a by-product of my light—it does not produce light.

Now you are hearing my voice, and yet you doubt. You wonder at these "thoughts"—which surprise you—and yet you cling to doubt. I will not remove these doubts by some spectacular miracle. I ask this of you—can you not, based on your experience of my love and power, *choose* to abandon doubt and embrace faith? Faith is humbling. Doubt is built on pride and independence. Think about that, and choose.

August Twentieth

Then the Lord said to him, "Take off the sandals from your feet, for the place where you are standing is holy ground."
—Acts 7:33

This listening time is a testing time. The cares of the day continue to intrude on your mind. Will you draw aside, take off your shoes, and stand on holy ground with me? Will you make space in your busy thoughts for my thoughts? I will not intrude—under ordinary circumstances. That is my way. So if you listen—if you will *keep listening*, you will hear my voice. I, the Lord your God, am speaking in the depths of your soul. Believe and hear.

August Twenty-first

The sacrifice acceptable to God is a broken spirit; a broken and contrite heart, O God, you will not despise.
—Psalm 51:17

A broken and contrite heart I do not despise. There are many ways in which the heart is broken—and there is always pain when it happens. Sometimes the pain lingers and even intensifies as time goes on. Such suffering can and must be offered up to me, my child, if its full benefit is to be realized. Let the pain of it be a continuing reminder that with the brokenness you have need for contriteness, humble repentance, meek acknowledgment, and full acceptance of your own sin. You can do this without condemnation, for I, the Lord, forgive and have forgiven. My forgiveness is absolute, but your appropriation and realization of it is dependent upon your degree of contriteness. A broken and contrite heart I do not despise.

August Twenty-second

"All things can be done for the one who believes. . . ."
"I believe; help my unbelief!"
—Mark 9:23b-24b

My word is alive in you, my child—active and life-giving. I am ever faithful to keep my promises. I cannot fail you, because I am God. Not only did I hear the cry of my people in Egypt, my ears are still open to their cry. You cannot yet understand my ways. They are hidden from your sight. But I have given you enough light for your faith walk. By trusting me where you cannot "see," your spirit grows in my likeness. Pray as the man prayed in today's gospel, "I believe; help my unbelief." I will answer that prayer.

Dear Father,
Help my unbelief!

August Twenty-third

. . . he saved us, not because of any works of righteousness . . .
but according to his mercy.
—Titus 3:5a

Springs of righteousness are flowing from my Spirit on the parched and thirsty ground of your soul. The paralyzing fear of being wrong clogs and blocks the flow of my Spirit and his life-giving power. It has nothing to do with your being "right." You have already been taught the truth of that. It has to do with inner release—inner release from the bondage of being right—from the fear of being wrong.

O my child, do you not see? My righteousness covers your petty "wrongness"—and washes it away in the sea of my love. When I ask you to obey, it is not "rightness" I seek, but the willing cooperation of your heart with my plan and path. The more you learn of me, the more you will see the glory and the freedom I offer you. As long as you stay in your demand to be "right" to cover up your "wrongness" or to make up for it, you will continue to block the flow from the springs of righteousness that flow from and by my Spirit. Your soul will remain parched and bare. The fruit of the Spirit will be dwarfed and scanty.

O the depths of my love are yours—if you will unblock the flow! It is not yet time for all the tears to be wiped away. Their cleansing, healing work is not done. Be of good cheer, and let them flow.

August Twenty-fourth

The LORD is near to all who call upon him,
to all who call on him in truth.
—Psalm 145:18

This day is a day of reckoning, of writing, of remembering. It is a day to cast aside your regrets about being wrong. They only hobble your feet and keep you from keeping time with my forward movement. It is not a day to be feared; you have spent much too much of your life in the shadow of fear. The sun is shining behind the overcast skies. You know that. Do not worry about the clouds.

It is also true in the realm of the Spirit. Uncertainty casts a cloud cover over your thoughts. But my light is still there, and you are able to walk in it—if you choose. Let the remembering today be of my mercies past. Let the reckoning be a measure of your thoughts and actions by my revealed and known will. It is not a day to be feared!

I woke this morning asking
God what He had for us today,
then read the above!
"The sun is shining behind the
overcast skies. Do not worry
about the clouds."

2017

August Twenty-fifth

There is no fear in love, but perfect love casts out fear; for fear has to do with punishment, and he who fears is not perfected in love.
—I John 4:18

I am the Lord who heals you. I am the God of hope. My word to you today, my child, is this: do not abandon hope! Your sight is very limited. Your interests are still very narrow. My view is larger and broader, and there is room for a lively hope in me. My sovereign power is still able to raise the dead. My promises are still valid. My love is still from everlasting to everlasting. So cling to the realities, the truth that you have been given. Let no disturbing thoughts dislodge them from your heart. I am the God of hope, and I give you the gift of hope—if you will claim it.

August Twenty-sixth

Wait for the L<small>ORD</small>; be strong, and let your heart take courage;
wait for the L<small>ORD</small>!
—Psalm 27:14

You shall seek me and find me when you seek me with all your heart. Your failure to find and hear comes from a divided and distracted heart. I will not supernaturally take away this condition. It is one that you must learn to hate, and to hate the bitter fruit it bears. When you are tired of it, and the spiritual lethargy that results, you will be willing to pay the price: *Then* you will find my presence and my reality. I don't curse your lethargy, but neither do I condone it.

August Twenty-seventh

When you search for me, you will find me;
if you seek me with all your heart. . . .
—Jeremiah 29:13

And now, my child, hear this word: your prayer is heard and you can cast all your cares on me. I will not fail you and will keep my word. My healing is still going on, and I have not forgotten you. Remember "the joy of the LORD is your strength" (Nehemiah 8:10b). So even now beforehand, rejoice in me. It *is* a good thing to rejoice and give thanks. You can never out-test my love and goodness.

August Twenty-eighth

. . . Jesus the pioneer and perfecter of our faith, who for the sake of the joy that was set before him endured the cross, disregarding its shame, and has taken his seat at the right hand of the throne of God.
—Hebrews 12:2

Is my arm shortened that it cannot save? Is my ear deaf to the cry of my children? You do not need to hide in shame over sins and mistakes of the past. I bore your shame on the cross that you might be spared. Yet you have lived long in shame and have not allowed my grace and mercy to cover you.

This present onslaught is an opportunity for you to "disregard the shame." This has been a weak point in you, and would have been even more harmful if I had not intervened. Claim the covering of my wings, and know that I am God. Claim the cleansing blood and seek deeper repentance. But "disregard the shame" of this attack. Have I not commanded thee?

August Twenty-ninth

"Whatever you ask for in prayer with faith, you will receive."
—Matthew 21:22

My dear child, you worry and fret about many foolish things, and thereby lose your peace. This is not necessary, for there is an abundance of peace available to you now, if you are open to it. When you allow your old nature to rise up in jealousy of your brethren—in fear of losing place or of being replaced—peace is sacrificed on the altar of pride. This is not a light thing but a serious condition that I choose to address. Together, my child, let us journey into a *new* place—a place of satisfaction and peace.

August Thirtieth

I will turn their mourning into joy, I will comfort them,
and give them gladness for sorrow.
—Jeremiah 31:13b

Hearken to my voice, O blessed child of mine. Hear the words of comfort that I speak within. Yes, I am the builder on ruins—the ruins that resulted from your wrong choices and wandering ways. These ruins are not only in your own life—they are also consequences you neither foresaw nor feared. I sanctify my name in those I claim, and I will be glorified in my work. I am the builder on ruins.

August Thirty-first

Do not let the wise boast in their wisdom, do not let the mighty boast
in their might, do not let the wealthy boast in their wealth; but let those
who boast boast in this, that they understand and know me, that I am the
LORD; I act with steadfast love, justice, and righteousness in the earth;
for in these things I delight, says the LORD.
—Jeremiah 9:23–24

I am not far—I have not gone away. You have separated yourself from me by
your thoughts and feelings. Your attitude toward my servant is abhorrent to
me, and it results in guilt in you. You are not called to be _____'s judge. You
are called to love her and respect her, even when you see her faults. Healing
is my business—pray and seek my love, my fatherly, paternal love, in your
heart. This love will wash away your bitter memories of the past and will
enable you to embrace fully my call on your life. Do not be afraid of this,
my child. My mercy is also toward you. You see, do you not, how much you
both need it?

SEPTEMBER

Speak, Lord, in the stillness,
　　　While I wait on Thee;
Hushed my heart to listen
　　　In expectancy.

Speak, O blessed Master,
　　　In this quiet hour,
Let me see Thy face, Lord,
　　　Feel Thy touch of power.

For the words Thou speakest-
　　　"They are life" indeed;
Living Bread from heaven,
　　　Now my spirit feed.

—E. May Grimes Crawford, 1864–1927

September First

Praise the LORD! Praise the LORD, O my soul! I will praise the LORD
as long as I live; I will sing praises to my God all my life long.
—Psalm 146:1–2

Praise is the key that unlocks the treasure store of my mercies. Numberless blessings are available to those who learn the secret of praise. As a flower unfolds before the sun, to receive its life-giving rays, so the soul opens before me through the act of praise. There is no life without light—and the soul that does not praise continues in its lifeless darkness.

Dwell in my life-giving light, my child, with a continuing attitude of praise and thanksgiving. Praise is the key that unlocks the treasure store of my mercies.

Keep praising the King!

September Second

*Is not my word like fire, says the LORD, and like a hammer
that breaks a rock in pieces?*
—Jeremiah 23:29

My word is like a hammer, breaking up the hardened crust of your heart.
I want you to have a tender, *feeling* heart, able to be touched with the pain
and sorrow of others. You have built up walls of deadness around your heart
to protect you from pain and to avoid looking weak. Your weakness, my
child, is my gift to you. Your strength is your rejection of that gift. There is
a world of difference between your strength and mine. I will show you that
difference when this breaking and hammering have done their work.

September Third

. . . but he said to me, "My grace is sufficient for you. . . ."
—2 Corinthians 12:9a

Yes, my child, I am here. "My grace is sufficient for you" and for all those you love. Trust me in this present circumstance. I have not forgotten to be gracious! Each uncertain hour is an opportunity for you to praise my goodness—even before you see the outworking of it before your eyes.

Call upon me more faithfully and fervently, not for my sake but for yours. I know your needs, and I am at work to meet them, but you need the exercise of prayer to be ready for my blessing. Do not think the time is wasted that you spend in prayer. Prayer is an antidote to pride and self-generated activity. Beware of the stress of busyness that crowds out the call to turn aside to be with me. Back to basics.

September Fourth

But the land you are crossing over to occupy,
is a land of hills and valleys. . . .
—Deuteronomy 11:11a

My dear child, the valleys as well as the hills are mine. Do not wonder that your path takes the lowlands as well as the high. I am with you in the desert as well as in the garden. To know this is life indeed.

Do not be afraid of tomorrow. All your tomorrows are known and planned by me—the Architect of time. I know the plans I have for you, plans of good and not of evil. Let your heart be open to my goodness.

September Fifth

. . . for it is well for the heart to be strengthened by grace.
—Hebrews 13:9b

Hearken to me, my child, and I will speak with you. Stop the busy, wandering thoughts and center your mind on me. Only thus can you hear a clear and undistorted word from me.

The work of renewal and revision is far from done. In each one of you, I am seeking to do a new thing. Yes, *seeking*, because I require the willing consent of my children in order to carry on my work within. This will not be easy, because an easier, less demanding way has been followed. Truth in the inward parts does not come without a price. Only those willing to pay the price will receive the prize.

Continue to seek me and my truth for your life. Do not let circumstances become an excuse to let up in this task. Have I not rewarded your efforts far beyond any expectation? Let these past months be a foundation for future faithfulness to our mutual goal—and the process by which you will move toward it.

September Sixth

Then Job answered the LORD: . . . "I had heard of you by the hearing of the ear, but now my eye sees you; therefore I despise myself, and repent in dust and ashes."
—Job 42:1, 5–6

The time of trial reveals the true condition of your soul. Its weaknesses are displayed to view and your lack of preparation is manifest. Therefore trials are necessary if you are to grow and progress in your life with me.

There is a healthy weakness that Job had to learn before me. Your human weakness before my divine majesty will always be a part of your reality. But there is an unhealthy weakness which seeks excuses for disobedience and sin. This you must be more careful to recognize and overcome. You *can* overcome this in the right way by wanting help and cooperating with my will. When your will is in harmony with mine, no power can resist or defeat you. That should be incentive enough to spur you on in this necessary battle.

September Seventh

*"So, for the sake of your tradition, you make void the word of
God. . . . '[I]n vain do they worship me, teaching human
precepts as doctrines' "*
Matthew 15:6, 9

I, the Lord your God, am speaking to you. My Spirit within carries my word
to my children. This is a living relationship. It is not made up of theories
and propositions, but of *life*—my life within your life.

In the past, you did not understand this, and in spite of the hunger of your
heart, you clung to ideas and doctrines. It is not that the doctrines were false,
but they could not provide what you needed and longed for without knowing
it. I have shown you in remembering glimpses of this hunger you felt.

Do not wonder at the reasons why I allowed the years to pass in this
way. Remember, my child, that I work with my children in wisdom and
mercy—and I know when to intervene and when to withhold. My view
of life is very different from yours. Only as you come to see with my vision
will you understand. In the meantime, trust me to give or withhold—in my
greater wisdom and love.

September Eighth

To set the mind on the flesh is death, but to set the
mind on the Spirit is life and peace.
Romans 8:6

In the quietness I speak. In the noise of your thoughts and words you cannot hear. Learn to be quiet. I have called you and commissioned you to a task too great for you. Only as you *listen* will you be able to fulfill your task. I will not forsake you nor let you bring harm to my work. But to fulfill your call, you *must* hear and heed what I say. Your fear of being wrong stops your ears from hearing. And *ephphatha*! (Mark 7:34)—be opened!

September Ninth

For I know that nothing good dwells within me, that is, in my flesh.
I can will what is right, but I cannot do it.
—Romans 7:18

You will continue to be led by thoughts that I put into your mind. You cannot always be sure such thoughts are from me, and you know the danger of confusing your opinions with my will. When your suggestions are refused, you find it humiliating and painful, because you are not free simply to release them into my keeping. Be bolder without demanding that every new thought "hit the target" and find approval. I will sort out the dross from the gold, and your obedience will work blessing both for you and for others.

September Tenth

. . . looking to Jesus the pioneer and perfecter of our faith, who for the
sake of the joy that was set before him endured the cross,
disregarding its shame. . . .
—Hebrews 12:2a

Yes, my child, the cross is a bitter thing. It was bitter for me when I bore it for you. You can never know how bitter it was, and you will never have to taste the full extent of its bitterness, because I bore it for you. Nevertheless, you must taste your part of its bitterness if you would be mine.

All my children have their part in this saving process—and come away cleansed and blessed. I came down from the cross a dead body—lifeless, ruined, and done for, as far as the powers of this world were concerned. But a deeper power had been challenged and did not know that on that very cross—that bitter cross—he was being unseated. So my victory beyond the cross is stamped on every cross I ask my children to endure. Because I live, no cross is as bitter as was mine. So do not fear any cross—you cannot be destroyed by it—only cleansed and made more fit for life in my kingdom.

September Eleventh

"Blessed are the poor in spirit. . . ."
—Matthew 5:3a

Humble your heart before me, my child, and let the poverty of your spirit make its plea to me. Presumption has long been a prevalent sin in your nature, and it is far from being eradicated. Your sense of impotent waiting is my weapon against this proud and haughty dimension in you. It is but a mild rebuke and is a guard against spiritual pride—the deadliest of all. When these delays come, do not lose heart. Repent of your impatience and humble your heart before me.

September Twelfth

For I am convinced that neither death, nor life, nor angels, nor rulers,
nor things present, nor things to come . . . will be able to separate us
from the love of God in Christ Jesus our Lord.
—Romans 8:38–39

I am the eternal One whose name is holy. I dwell in the high and holy place, and also with those who are humble in heart. Your afflictions are sent in mercy, my child, and were not designed to destroy you. Rather they are sent to humble and train you in godly trust. You still have much to learn, because you withdraw from me in your fear and imagine yourself alone. O foolish one! Nothing can separate you from my love—not even your withdrawal. You suffer needlessly when you choose fear instead of faith. Learn, learn!

September Thirteenth

. . . and be kind to one another, tenderhearted, forgiving one another, as
God in Christ has forgiven you.
—Ephesians 4:32

My forgiveness must extend to every hurt and wrong you *feel* you have sustained. Unforgiveness will block the flow of my life, and will rob you of the blessing I want you to know. Let every hurt be an occasion of learning from me how to forgive. Put down absolutely and resolutely all thoughts of "evening things up." Accept the pain of not being able to redress the situation. That, at its best, would only "treat the wound of my people carelessly" (Jeremiah 8:11a). Let my healing touch the wound, and remember, my child, there are other wounded souls besides yours. Pray to see clearly, much more clearly than you now see, how you have wounded another. Let go the demand to be heard and accepted. Inasmuch as lies within *you*, live peaceably with all. That is all I ask of you—and it is enough.

September Fourteenth

I have no greater joy than this, to hear that my children
are walking in truth.
—3 John 4

Out of the darkness of fear I invite you into the light of faith. Out of the darkness of self, I invite you into the light of my glory. When you turn your thoughts to *you*, you enter a dark, windowless room—a kind of solitary cell. Uncertainties plague you, and every small pain gets magnified because of what it might become. Yet you are not in prison—except by your own choosing. The key that opens the door and lets the light of my presence flood your soul is *praise*. It is not "begging prayers" but "returning thanks" that turns the key.

It gives me no joy to see my children in their own self-chosen darkness. This brings me no honor or satisfaction. It was not for this that my child gave his life. It was to draw to me a free people with changed hearts and joyful spirits. The work of redemption has been done. Why grovel as though the battle had not been won?

Out of your darkness, I invite you, my child, into my light. Where I am, there is light.

September Fifteenth

But to one who without works trusts him who justifies the
ungodly, such faith is reckoned as righteousness.
—Romans 4:5

My living water I freely give to those who seek my face. My grace is not confined to the worthy. Rather it is designed for those whose only claim is their unworthiness. I do not ask my children to grovel before me. When you are convicted of your sin, when you become painfully aware of your human appetite for the lower elements of your nature, what I desire is an inward turning to my light, my face. This is not to make light of your wrongness, but to make *Light* of it, turning darkness to light.

It is at this point my children often become confused and veer into desert paths of their own choosing. Condemnation and fruitless effort do not make saints. Pride waits to ride in behind these substitutes for saving grace. My glory is obscured behind the subtle and secret pride in the effort put forth to make up for the feeling of condemnation. Tread carefully here, that you do not fall into the trap—the empty cistern—when living water flows freely from my throne of grace.

September Sixteenth

In God, whose word I praise, in God I trust; I am not afraid;
what can flesh do to me?
—Psalm 56:4

My dear child, your doubting of my goodness is a sin and offense against me. How can you doubt? How can you doubt after all the ways I have shown you my mercy? I have fed and clothed you, led you along a path that you did not know nor understand. I have guarded your home and dwelling—and your children. There is no end to my faithfulness. Yet you come cringing, fearing, and full of your petty sin. Wash yourself and make yourself clean! Put behind you all these doubts and fears and repent of them—for my love and my grace do not ebb and flow with the changing tide. Gird yourself for the tasks ahead, and do not flinch from them. I will supply your need day by day. Only believe and receive—and doubt no more!

September Seventeenth

Happy are those whose transgression is forgiven, whose sin is covered.
—Psalm 32:1

My child, accept my pardon for your many failures, and go on in my strength for the rest of your journey. Continue to give thanks for my provisions and my heavenly watchcare. Build on the solid rock of my sovereign grace, and never let yourself be moved from the foundation. Redeem the time, and be faithful unto death.

September Eighteenth

My dear child, I have no delight in the suffering of my people. I allow it only for their eternal good. Blessed are those who turn to me in their trouble, for I am a God of mercy and compassion. The valleys through which I call you to go need not frighten you. The shadows and darkness are only for a time. Let your faith grow strong when darkness comes. Faith will overcome where daylight cannot prevail. Suffering purges away the growth of self—if you let it do its work. There are two ways in which I turn it to good: by its pruning and by my healing. In both ways I bring blessing to my chosen ones.

September Nineteenth

Many are the afflictions of the righteous, but the LORD
rescues them from them all.
—Psalm 34:19

My dear child, be content with my love and be attentive to my correction. Know that they come from my fatherly care, the Shepherd's care for his sheep. Let them turn your heart and mind in my direction instead of your own willful way. I will lead you in the right paths, and refresh you by the still waters of comfort. Only do not despise my disciplining nor be discouraged at my corrections. They are necessary in your spiritual growth and progress. Bless my name and my ways, even when they confound your understanding—*especially* when they confound your understanding.

September Twentieth

I will be like the dew to Israel.
—Hosea 14:5a

In the dew of the morning, I come down to refresh and revive your soul. In the light of the morning, I dispel the darkness of your mind. In the joy of the morning, I dispel the sadness of your spirit. You do not make these things happen. They are my gift and my work in your soul. "I am about to do a new thing" (Isaiah 43:19a), and it is my will that you be blessed in it. Bless me in your heart—sanctify my name within your heart. Turn aside from every wicked thought and seek me more faithfully and more frequently as your day goes on. Weariness comes, not from fighting, but from surrendering to the flatteries of the adversary.

September Twenty-first

Be still before the LORD, and wait patiently for him. . . .
—Psalm 37:7a

Those who wait before me here cannot be disappointed, for I, the Lord, keep my appointments. Waiting may seem tedious, even confusing to you, my child, but *think!* Consider how long I have waited for you. It is not my reluctance but the massive barrier of *thought-habit* that keeps our communication from starting more easily. Waiting and repentance are good companions at this point in your journey.

September Twenty-second

I appeal to you therefore, brothers and sisters, by the mercies of God. . . .
—Romans 12:1a

O my dear child, the wonders of my love surround you on every side. As yet you do not see or recognize many of them, because you still look on the outward appearance. Why are you afraid to look more deeply? Do you not yet know that my intention for you is love? You cannot fully and effectively minister my reality to others if you are still afraid of seeing my full purpose and embracing it. You resist still in your heart against the full expression of my will. And this resistance separates you from me. We cannot walk closely together when you pull back—afraid, accusing, rebellious. O my dear child, by my past mercies I appeal to you—yes, I the Lord, *appeal* to you: trust me and do not separate yourself from the fullness of my love.

September Twenty-third

My steps have held fast to your paths, my feet have not slipped.
—Psalm 17:5

My dear child, my word to you today is this: walk in my love, as I have loved you. My love lays down a safe path for your feet. You do not know the dangers that surround you on every side, but I chart a safe course through them, and bid you walk there. The path is clear, and will open moment by moment as you have need.

September Twenty-fourth

So Peter got out of the boat, started walking on the water, and came toward Jesus. But when he noticed the strong wind, he became frightened, and beginning to sink, he cried out, "Lord, save me!" Jesus immediately reached out his hand and caught him, saying to him, "You of little faith, why did you doubt?"
—Matthew 14:29b–31

My child, I am with you always. You are never alone, even when you feel alone. The depths are mine, as well as the heights. No waters can drown those who are in my care. Too many times you look at the "waters"—the circumstances that contain pain and seem to threaten your very life. But these are trials of your trust in me. If you do not trust me then, when can you? Do not waste the dry times, the lonely times when I seem far away. Let them acquaint you with the deeper truth that "underneath are the everlasting arms" (Deuteronomy 33:27b NIV).

September Twenty-fifth

Into your hand I commit my spirit; you have redeemed me,
O LORD, faithful God.
—Psalm 31:5

Go about the day calmly and without hurry. In the midst of much bustle, keep a quiet spirit. Let your word of encouragement be a source of peace to others. Be generous in your encouragement and expressions of appreciation. Cement relations with the bond of love. I will be with you and remind you of this.

September Twenty-sixth

I do not occupy myself with things too great and too marvelous for me.
But I have calmed and quieted my soul. . . .
—Psalm 131:1b–2a

Yes, child, you may lean on me. My heart is open to you; my ear is attuned to your cry. Do not marvel that this is so, and do not wonder about "things too great for you." My mercies never run short, they endure forever. Those who know my name, those whom I have called by name, are vessels of mercy. Taste here the sweetness of my fatherly love. Give over your understanding and receive it as a little child. The wilderness way is hard. Welcome here, my child. You may lean on me.

September Twenty-seventh

Let the words of my mouth and the meditation of my heart be acceptable to you, O LORD, my rock and my redeemer.
—Psalm 19:14

I am with you always, even to the end. My gentle voice is easily drowned out with the cluttering of your own thoughts and earthly concerns. Listen more intently—do not grow discouraged or give up. This is all a part of maturing in me—and a preparation for the future.

I am putting my words in your mouth and in your mind. By faith, you can receive them, speak and hear them. Do not worry about getting them "right." That is pride. I will not allow you to stray too far. Trust me.

September Twenty-eighth

Love does no wrong to a neighbor; therefore, love is the
fulfilling of the law.
—Romans 13:10

There is no fear in love. As your love for me grows, you will find that fear lessens. My wrath is against sin—not against persons. When you persist in sin, my wrath will be felt. But it is meant to turn you away from sin and its consequent, fear—to my welcoming love. This is not sentimentality. It is an eternal truth.

Concentrate, therefore, on my unfathomable love. Your heart has long responded to this dimension of the gospel, but your growth was stunted in many ways. It is time to move on, trusting me each step of the way—to open doors, to shed light on the path, to lead, to turn, and to reward your faltering steps of obedience. Let the latter part of your journey be better than the former. The old has passed away. Let it be. Come with me, my child, and learn love's way. It is a good way, and blessed are those who walk in it.

September Twenty-ninth

Gracious is the LORD, and righteous; our God is merciful. The LORD
protects the simple; when I was brought low, he saved me.
Psalm 116:5–6

My dear child, you worry about things too high for you. You delve into mysteries that must remain mysteries—and you are not satisfied to leave them at that. Rest your mind in the simplicity of the faith I have planted in you, and do not fret about these larger questions. Leave them to me to sort out. You have all the light you need to walk with me day by day. That is enough.

September Thirtieth

The scripture says, "No one who believes in him will be put to shame."
—Romans 10:11

My child, when I speak, your fear of "getting it wrong" interferes with our communication. You must not wait for some overwhelming assurance that you are really hearing, but follow more readily the "small voice" within. I, too, want there to be the sweet goings in and out between us, the comfortable relationship that allows that sense of rest. You still hold me at arm's length—afraid of looking foolish to others—afraid of being confounded. Have I not given you enough evidence that you can move on?

OCTOBER

Open my ears that I may hear
 Voices of truth thou sendest clear;
And while the wave-notes fall on my ear,
 Everything false will disappear;
Silently now I wait for Thee,
 Ready, my God, thy will to see.
Open my ears, illumine me,
 Spirit divine.

—Clara H. Fiske Scott, 1841–1897

October First

"I made your name known to them, and I will make it known, so that the love with which you have loved me may be in them, and I in them."
—John 17:26

I will walk with you, all the way, my child. I do not forsake those who put their trust in me, however weak and wavering their faith may be. Few, very few, are strong in faith. The effects of sin and rebellion linger on in the soul even after new life has begun. But I claim as mine all that the Father has given me, and I do not abandon those who are mine.

Put away this faithless fear you have been entertaining. I will be with you. What is there to fear with me at hand? Claim the promise, child, whenever these fears assault your mind! Turn the moment into a blessing by recognizing and resisting the adversary in my power. Be prepared to be a blessing, and you will be blessed. I repeat again: there is nothing to fear with me at your side.

October Second

And he was amazed at their unbelief.
—Mark 6:6a

This is the day of miracles. My power and love will combine and my glory will be shown. Awaken your heart, be expectant, not reluctant, before my promise. I can do exceedingly abundantly above all you ask or think. You need to stretch your faith, my child, instead of nursing puny, negative doubts and fears. Faith still moves mountains—faith and prayer. Faith is borne on the wings of prayer. This is what you need to practice—faith-filled praying, expectant, eager, and confident praying. My heart is gladdened when my children pray this way. Don't be afraid of believing too much. Be afraid of limiting my work and cheating my glory by believing too little. I love to reward a subdued, believing heart, a faith that has been tried and not found wanting. Pray for such a faith and I will give it to you; and then it is yours to guard and use for my glory. Awaken, my child, awaken your heart!

October Third

"Everyone then who hears these words of mine and acts on them will be like a wise man who built his house on rock."
—Matthew 7:24

I am that solid Rock. There is no other beside me. I am the sure foundation of all your life and hope. Your rock-like mind is not the solid Rock. It is the rubble of years of misuse. Yet it is hard, and you often get stuck in it and think you are firmly standing on me. O my dear child, I am so much greater than these little "chunks of opinion" you stand on so bravely and with so much pride. Your rightness is not your salvation. I am your salvation, but you can neither live it out nor even realize it unless you are willing to lose—to lose. You will lose face in your mind but nowhere else. Work today on being willing to lose—not just outwardly, but inwardly, and with a good heart and spirit. It is not as hard as you think!

October Fourth

While he was at Bethany in the house of Simon the leper, as he sat at the table, a woman came with an alabaster jar of very costly ointment of nard, and she broke open the jar and poured the ointment on his head.
—Mark 14:3

My dear child, do not forget that I love you. Do not heedlessly trample on my love by doubting it or forgetting it. My love is a purifier of motives, the inner hidden workings of the heart. It does cleanse and burn and consume the lower passions of your nature when you keep it as a peculiar treasure and gift. Everything that I ask of you and everything that I allow to come into your life is rooted in my divine love. You cannot measure or understand or comprehend my love—but you can accept it in a way you never have. The woman in the Gospel reading had accepted my love. Simon had not. Where is the alabaster box of ointment in your life? Break it, my child, and be amply blessed.

October Fifth

So Jonah set out and went to Nineveh, according to the word of the LORD.
—Jonah 3:3a

Come to my side where rivers of mercy flow freely. Cleansing and renewal are ever to be found here. Let your tears mingle with mine for all that is and has been amiss in your life. Let the tears be of sorrow and of joy. The three days spent in the deep were days of change for Jonah. Even though his nature and opinions still rose up, nevertheless he obeyed my voice and went to Nineveh with my word. I charge you, my child, to be a faithful bearer of my word. Do not allow your fear of the disapproval of others make you unfaithful. You cannot enter fully into my joy and strength unless and until you risk that disapproval in order to deliver my word as faithfully as you can. I tell you that I am your shield and great reward! You did not choose me, but I have chosen you to be a bearer of my word. O my child, do not fail yourself and me!

October Sixth

He does not deal with us according to our sins;
nor repay us according to our iniquities.
—Psalm 103:10

No, my child, you are not worthy that I should come under your roof. My presence in you is not based on your worthiness but on my grace. I am he who "is merciful and gracious" (Psalm 103:8). Otherwise, my creation would long ago have been destroyed.

I am with you in your struggle against your fallen nature. I have redeemed you. I have called you by name. You are mine. But your old nature will not fit in my Kingdom of love and righteousness. It is a twisted and perverted nature and must die. Daily deaths are part of this dying. Do not cringe from them. They are from me.

October Seventh

[N]one of those who take refuge in him will be condemned.
—Psalm 34:22b

It is not necessary, my child, to have feelings of any particular kind in these listening times. The important thing is steadiness, faithfulness, perseverance. My will and desire are unchanging—make no mistake about that. I have declared it to all my children, and would that they would believe and act on it. But "let anyone with ears listen" (Mathew 11:15). I am more than ready to speak. Your difficulty lies in part in feeling that it will be necessary to have certain *feelings* before you can trust what you hear. Trust more, and do not be so afraid of being wrong!

October Eighth

Why are you cast down, O my soul, and why are you disquieted within
me? Hope in God; for I shall again praise him, my help and my God.
—Psalm 43:5

I am the Lord your God. Look for me in all that comes to pass today. View
the circumstances as my will—and do not struggle against them. Be at peace
within, my child, for I am he who brings the gift of peace. When you are
sad within and do not understand your own emotions, you distress yourself,
and stay stressed inside when you could be resting in my goodness and love.
My will for you is to seek and find a heavenly rest—a rest that goes beyond
your outer circumstances and is not disturbed by them.

October Ninth

But exhort one another every day, as long as it is called "today," so that none of you may be hardened by the deceitfulness of sin.
—Hebrews 3:13

The breaking must continue. The hardness is not all gone. A soft and tender heart is what you need. You have calcified your heart for many years, and it is my will that this damage be undone. A person after my own heart is one whose heart is sensitive to the pain of others, not wrapped up in saving himself from pain and suffering. Seek that, my child, if you would come after me. Hate the hardness that spares a momentary pain but inflicts greater pain on others without thinking about it. I will not fail you. You do not have to do it alone.

October Tenth

*Is not this the fast that I choose: to loose the bonds of injustice,
to undo the thongs of the yoke, to let the oppressed
go free, and to break every yoke?*
—Isaiah 58:6

What do I require of you, my child? I lay on you no burden but that which belongs to your peace. My requirements may seem irksome to you. I know that they often do. But they are sent for your healing and growth, and to make you what you tell me you want to be—a blessing to others. I do not deal with you in isolation, but with all the connections of your life. Together they form the matrix of my mercies, and I use them all for my purposes.

October Eleventh

By faith we understand that the worlds were prepared by the word of God,
so that what is seen was made from things that are not visible.
—Hebrews 11:3

My love for you is new every morning. Let your love for me be renewed in this meeting. Put the fears and shadows of the night behind you, and see me in the unfolding of the day.

This world extends in time by my permission and my will. Ages and eons and epochs—these are but moments in eternity. I have created you and called you to live in eternity. You cannot grasp or understand what that means. But you can embrace my love anew every day—every moment you are given to live. In this way you are entering eternity even while confined in time. Do not waste these little moments—seek to be renewed in your love for me. Redeem the time. Fight the battle of faith.

October Twelfth

Indeed, the word of God is living and active, sharper than any two-edged sword, piercing until it divides soul from spirit, joints from marrow; it is able to judge the thoughts and intentions of the heart.
—Hebrews 4:12

My word is near. It is more sure than the beating of your heart. It is a fire to burn away the dross of folly in your soul. It is warmth to kindle a saving love. It is light to scatter the dark shadows of your fear-generated night. Rejoice in my word, for through it I raise you to your intended dignity as a child of God. Bow before it, for through it I show you the lowliness of your fallen state. Be a hearer, my dear child, and a doer. Heed and obey the word I speak—and enjoy life abundant.

October Thirteenth

You will not fear the terror of the night,
or the arrow that flies by day. . . .
—Psalm 91:5

The night seasons, my child, are the seasons of battle. "You will not fear the terror of the night . . . or the destruction that wastes at noonday" (Psalm 91:5a, 6b). Others before you have endured the assaults of the enemy that came in the darkness. But in me, darkness and light are both alike—for I am the inner Light that dispels the power of the outer darkness.

When you give ground to fearful thoughts and vain imaginations, you open the floodgates to your adversary. Your only recourse is to flee to me. In this case, fleeing is fighting. You are no match for his wiles, and you need to stay very close to me if you would know my victorious power. I will help you, but I will not force you to come to me.

Remember, my child, your pride—your spiritual pride—is being dealt with in these night battles. You are not a hero—just a frightened child whom I love.

October Fourteenth

"I will show you what someone is like who comes to me, hears my words, and acts on them. That one is like a man building a house, who dug deeply and laid the foundation on rock. . . ."
—Luke 6:47–48a

My dear child, the Rock on which you build your hope must be me alone. All other foundations and footings will crumble and give way. You have not been aware of how false and weak some of your "footings" are. I have assured you that I will not leave nor forsake you—yet you have so relied on these other foundations that panic replaced peace, and fear replaced faith. Do not waste these experiences. Do not repress the memory of them as you go on. It is my love and mercy that led you into and out of the circumstances, and my love and mercy will open new opportunities for you to reject the false foundations and choose this one firm Foundation—the Rock of Ages. Repent and believe the Good News.

October Fifteenth

Now all the Athenians and the foreigners living there would spend their time in nothing but telling or hearing something new.
—Acts 17:21

Truth is a spring of living water. It does not grow stale or trite, even though the verbal expressions may seem time-worn. Truth carries life-giving properties for the soul, and without these properties the soul languishes and shrivels. Cherish and hunger for truth, my child, for it shall make you free. Whether it is pleasant or bitter, its effect is health-bringing.

Many souls run shipwreck in their pursuit of *new* thoughts and ideas. They lose their devotion to the truth they have once known. They are fascinated and dazzled by the entertaining effects of newness and surprise. Be careful in your seeking to hold on to the truth that I have entrusted to you. Beware of boredom, for it is a sign that you are seeking a false goal—something that will crowd out the good entrusted to you. Don't worry about being original. Let me take care of that!

October Sixteenth

... *bearing with one another in love, making every effort to maintain the unity of the Spirit in the bond of peace.*
—Ephesians 4:2b–3

My child, today is a gift of my love. Your very life is a gift of my love for you. I want you to live as a child of love. I want you to reflect that love in your relations with others. Since I am the source and giver of life, there is no shortage of supply. Only if you interject your self-driven life in these relationships will the flow of my life be impeded. Make the day brighter around you by denying your darkness and letting my light shine through you. Today is a gift of my love. Live as a child of my love.

October Seventeenth

"If you then, who are evil, know how to give good gifts to your children,
how much more will your Father in heaven give
good gifts to those who ask him!"
—Matthew 7:11

Expect good and not evil from my hand, my child. Would you give your children something that would hurt or harm them? How much more is my love and mercy toward you! Expect good—that is the faith that moves mountains. That is the faith that unlocks closed doors. That is the faith that overcomes the world. Simple? Yes, my child, for your life turns on such simple truth. You either look to me with expectant faith, or you look with accusing thoughts. You bring your needs, knowing from all your past experiences that my help does not fail. And in your asking, you choose whom you shall believe: the accuser or the faithful One. It's that simple. Expect good and not evil from my hand.

October Eighteenth

Let us therefore no longer pass judgment on one another,
but resolve instead never to put a stumbling block or
hindrance in the way of another.
—Romans 14:13

Your fickle and unsteady affection is a grievous fault. You can become more stable and steadfast if you will give up judging others harshly and yourself softly. You want to love me with your whole heart? Then hear and heed what I say. The path to steadfastness involves crucifying your hard and unmerciful nature. Grace abounds for this to happen. Do not fear to let it come to pass.

October Nineteenth

"Why are you afraid? Have you still no faith?"
—Mark 4:40b

This is my word for you today: hear and do not fear. Draw near and do not fear. Be of good cheer and do not fear. The winds and waves still obey my will—and that includes all the storms that arise in your life. If you will listen more carefully and obey more readily, you will not be terrified by the billows and waves of life. Keep faith with this secret place. Again I say, keep faith!

October Twentieth

*Great peace have those who love your law; nothing
can make them stumble.*
—Psalm 119:165

With my peace I bless those who seek it. It is found in unexpected places and times, for it is not a peace as the world knows peace. My peace is found in surrender. To the extent that you agree with my will, you experience that peace. It may be in the midst of uncertainty, even of pain, but when your will is united with mine, peace follows. It cannot be otherwise.

Stress grows from your vain attempt to control your future. It comes from believing that you know the way you should go. O foolish one! I am the Way and I know the way. To surrender is to *give in* to my way over yours. Since my way is life and peace, does it not make sense to choose it? Those who love my way have great peace.

October Twenty-first

And many false prophets wall arise and lead many astray.
—Matthew 24:11

I am truth, and I am life. The words that I speak to you come with the nature of truth. Never fear truth, my child, for it is life-giving and healing, even when it is most painful. Deception and delusions are ever ready to bend or twist the truth so as to destroy its effectiveness. Remember this: deception is death-dealing; truth is life-bringing. The song and the joy in your heart must always be grounded in the truth. Otherwise they are exercises in delusion and bring no life. I hear your prayers, my child, and I again assure you that your prayers will be and are being answered. Great things have yet to unfold in my purpose. It is my grace to allow you to witness them and share in the faith-fulfillment they are intended to bring. Open your heart, then, to my truth and my life.

October Twenty-second

Cast your burden on the LORD.
"Take my yoke upon you. . . .
For my yoke is easy, and my burden is light."
—Psalm 55:22a and Matthew 11:29a, 30

Cast your burden on me, and take my burden on you. Your burden is too heavy for you, my child. It is laden with sins past, old guilt, many fears, and unwholesome ambitions. There must be a daily "casting" of this burden upon me, or it will grow heavier and heavier, weighing you down and hindering your journey. Ask my Spirit's searchlight to show you where you need to face any sin, repent, and be freed.

Take my burden in place of yours. My burden of care, of love for others who may never return yours in kind, of faithfulness in prayer and the burden of faith, of believing where you cannot see. Accept *this* burden, my child, and travel light!

October Twenty-third

Teach me good judgment and knowledge,
for I believe in your commandments.
—Psalm 119:66

Hearken to me, my dear child, and listen attentively. Learn to look with the eyes of the spirit beyond the outer shell. Let your thoughts and your words aim at what lies hidden from the natural view, and do not be confused by it. I will give you the discernment you need in order to minister life. Remember that my love and care go beyond any immediate problems. Pray that you may see with me the long view—the good to which I am leading each child of mine. Too much attention on the single incident can cloud that vision and cause unnecessary problems.

October Twenty-fourth

". . . it is your Father's good pleasure to give you the k ingdom."
—Luke 12:32b

No one waits for me in vain. I am he who keeps promises. Do not let yourself grow weary when I seem to delay. There is good reason for it, even if you never know what it is. Trust is not built on knowledge of details. Trust is in the character of the One in whom you choose to believe. I have given you more than ample evidence of who I am, my child. I am not playing games with you as a pawn. He who waits for me will not be confounded. That is my sovereign promise. Be at peace.

October Twenty-fifth

*. . . for it is God who is at work in you, enabling you both
to will and to work for his good pleasure.*
—Philippians 2:13

Your children are in my care. I will never let them go. You have seen already
how I can change circumstances and move in the hidden depths of hearts.
Never doubt my faithfulness. Never let circumstances shake your faith that
I will keep my solemn word. Keep praying and keep believing. There will yet
be a happy issue from all your afflictions.

October Twenty-sixth

The LORD is gracious and merciful, slow to anger and abounding in steadfast love. The LORD is good to all, and his compassion is over all that he has made.
—Psalm 145:8–9

I have told you that the year ahead will bring many surprises. Not all of them will be pleasant, but *all* of them will be in the compass of my mercy. They will bring blessing, and I want you to be prepared to look for and recognize the blessing.

Discount the nay-saying spirits. No worthwhile achievement is ever accomplished without struggle and questions. Present vision is but partial and very incomplete. Keep open to have your eyes refocused and the vision made clearer. I am still revealing my plan, even in the delays and the necessary changes. But do not lose heart. I will not fail you.

October Twenty-seventh

The LORD is just in all his ways, and kind in all his doings.
—Psalm 145:17

The hollow of my hand is not always easy to recognize. My leadings may seem strange and even unloving to you. But I have kept you safe from the enemy's designs and have tolerated your rebellion against my will. Your murmurings and inward complaints are not hidden from me. I know where you are safest and most blessed—you do not, and it is my grace that holds you back.

October Twenty-eighth

Every generous act of giving, with every perfect gift, is from
above, coming down from the Father of lights, with whom
there is no variation or shadow due to change.
—James 1:17

I have promised, and I will fulfill. I have spoken and I will do what I have said. There is neither variableness nor shadow of turning with me. All things are present to my view, and my wisdom encompasses every circumstance and event. The shadows in your life are cast by your own self, standing between my light and the concern you have. By stepping aside, and allowing my light to shine on the situation, you will be able to see and understand much that now remains dark and uncertain.

October Twenty-ninth

Let us therefore approach the throne of grace with boldness, so that we
may receive mercy and find grace to help in time of need.
—Hebrews 4:16

I am here, my dear child, even though you do not see or "feel" my presence.
Your fears and your tears are not hidden from my eyes. These "low" times
where there is no feeling of victory and little of joy are all part of my perfect
plan. I do not cause them in you, but it is my will to use them for your
good. They penetrate beneath the shallow and surface joy you would choose,
and drive your roots deeper into the mystery of my suffering love. Stay close
to me, my child. I am very near to you.

October Thirtieth

So neither the one who plants nor the one who waters is anything,
but only God who gives the growth.
—1 Corinthians 3:7

I plant and move and pluck up. I water and bring forth fruit in its season. But tending the plant I leave in part to you. The necessary pruning I bring about in various ways, but I ask for your willing assent. "Let it be with me according to your word" (Luke 1:38b), as did Mary of Nazareth. It was as hard for her to say yes to my plan as it has ever been for you. You can see how I used her assent to further my redemptive design. You cannot see how I will make use of yours. The pruning is first for your own sake, and then to make useful in my kingdom the fruit your life will bear.

October Thirty-first

. . . the work of each builder will become visible, for the Day will
disclose it, because it will be revealed with fire, and the
fire will test what sort of work each has done.
—I Corinthians 3:13

Insights are given by my Spirit to enable you to walk more faithfully in the path I have laid out for you. Past faithlessness has cost you many a victory, and you have suffered loss—throwing in hay, wood, and stubble, when I offered you gold, silver, and precious stones. You have excused yourself from hard places when you *could* have *stood* and served me. Do try to learn from the past so that in the time of testing, you will make better choices. "No arm so weak but may do service here" (Jane Laurie Borthwick). This includes yours. All you risk is a little pain—an unpleasant incident, the threat of losing someone's favor and good opinion. Let your new insight work for you, my child.

NOVEMBER

Breathe through the
heats of our desire
    thy coolness and thy balm;
  Let sense be dumb, let flesh retire,
    speak through the earthquake,
wind and fire,
    O still small voice of calm.

—John G. Whittier, 1807–1892

November First

There is therefore now no condemnation for those who are in Christ Jesus.
—Romans 8:1

Know this, my child, there is no condemnation for those whose trust is in me. My righteousness covers the wrongness that belongs to your old nature. My sacrifice of myself is your "ticket" to heaven—not any rightness of your own. You still recoil and draw back when confronted with the "badness" of what your human nature is without my intervening grace. You still struggle to find evidence of "goodness" in yourself, and this becomes bondage instead of freedom.

Relax and let go. I am still with you. Do not try to reason everything out, but trust in my mercy.

Trust in God's mercy!!

November Second

When Jesus saw her, he called her over and said, "Woman,
you are set free from your ailment."
—Luke 13:12

Take this day as it comes, as my gift to you and those you love. They are mine,
and my love for them is greater than yours. I know their inmost thoughts and
their deepest wounds. I know where they have hardened themselves against
further hurt. I am the Lord who heals. I am the repairer of breaches—the
builder on ruins. Just as the woman was bound and bent-over for eighteen
years and could not stand up straight, so my children become bound with
troublesome spirits of unforgiveness and hurt and remain crippled until my
freeing touch releases them to new life. Do not be surprised at my goodness.
Do not blink at the way I achieve my purpose. Trust in me, O you of little
faith, that my promises will be fulfilled. Take this day as it comes. Rejoice,
trust, hope—in me.

November Third

Let the righteous rejoice in the LORD and take refuge in him.
Let all the upright in heart glory.
—Psalm 64:10

Abide in me, my child, and I abide in you. I am ever ready to inhabit a heart that seeks me. I am ever ready to fellowship with a spirit who knows its need of me. I do not look for cringing, frightened children. That image belongs to the dark side of your nature. I look for free and open communion with those who have accepted my redemption and rejoice in it. Oh, that my people could see and understand my ways! They would not come crawling as beggars, but running as little children to a loving father or mother. That is the relationship that brings joy to my heart, because it is grounded in the truth!

November Fourth

But God, who is rich in mercy, out of the great love with
which he loved us even when we were dead through
our trespasses, made us alive together with Christ. . . .
—Ephesians 2:4–5a

The great abundance of my mercy exceeds all your needs. There is an unending and ever-flowing supply for those who turn to me. I am the divine Giver.
It is my joy to bestow blessings—and your joy in receiving them gladdens
my heart. Do not dwell on the negative thoughts that arise. Quickly confess
your sin and turn from it with hope quickened by my promises. The great
abundance of my mercy exceeds all your needs.

November Fifth

For my thoughts are not your thoughts, nor are your
ways my ways, says the LORD.
—Isaiah 55:8

Yes, my child, my mercies are beyond numbering, and they are new every morning. It is my pleasure to do good things to my children and for my children. Just as you desire good for yours, I seek good for mine.

My ways are not your ways and thereby you often become confused. You think of me as one like yourself—but my love is a pure love, not contaminated with self and sin and guilt as is yours. So, as my love and my ever-new mercies operate in your life and the life of your loved ones, learn to *entrust* them and yourself to my tender care. Only then can you know the "peace which surpasses all understanding" (Philippians 4:7a), for your peace will not depend on your understanding.

November Sixth

But you are a chosen race, a royal priesthood, a holy nation, God's own people, in order that you may proclaim the mighty acts of him who called you out of darkness into his marvelous light.
—I Peter 2:9

I make the light of my face to shine upon you. I look upon you with mercy and compassion, because I know who you are. Do not look on yourself with disdain or despising. You are the work of my hands, and too much negative attention on your failures and faults is an exercise in self. There is a better way—rejoicing in my saving work, rejoicing in what I have accomplished for you, rejoicing in my incarnation and in my complete identification with you. I became what you are without sinning, in order to lead you toward what you are yet to be. The light of my countenance still shines upon you, and the path before us still leads to your true destiny. So do not whine or repine. *Rejoice* in me, and all I have given you.

November Seventh

Render serving with enthusiasm, as to the Lord and not to men and women, knowing that whatever good we do, we will receive the same again from the Lord. . . .
—Ephesians 6:7–8a

You are still too concerned about what others think of you. This is a serious block in your relationship with me. It distorts your perception and hobbles your feet. I would not have you to be unmindful and deaf to what others say to you, but you magnify their input to such a degree that it does not do its intended work. You are seeking life in their good opinion of you, and you interpret their negative words as destruction rather than helpful correction of some fault.

This, my child, is immature behavior. Part of your hidden design in all your work is the demand that it be accepted and approved. Take courage and trust me. I will not fail you!

November Eighth

The LORD has established his throne in the heavens,
and his kingdom rules over all.
—Psalm 103:19

In my will for you there is much still to be learned. The horizons of your mind are still too narrow and confined. Your heart must become larger and freer if you are to follow my plan for you. I have allowed you to see some of the vastness of my creation and to see the results of my patient process in creation. Let these images challenge the smallness and pettiness that is natural to you. Come out of the rigid narrowness of your nature and indulge yourself in the greatness of mine.

My plans for you are not yet fulfilled. Embrace each day with a new enthusiasm and hope. Fight against the fear and negative outlook that lurks beneath the surface of your most positive days. My kingdom *will* come and my will *shall* prevail—so live and pray with a new confidence. This is pleasing in my sight—and more pleasing by far than cringing, fearful prayer that doubts my fatherly care!

November Ninth

We must no longer be children, tossed to and fro and blown about by
every wind of doctrine . . . by their craftiness in deceitful scheming.
—Ephesians 4:14

Put aside your petty thoughts and ways, my child, and allow your soul to be enlarged before my greatness. There are many mysteries you cannot understand, for you are finite, dust. Yet I have loved you and called you forth from nothingness to share my glory and my love. This mystery will always remain a source of joy and wonder.

Do not try to reason out how my purposes unfold. Keep close to the central truths you have been shown, and do not wander into vain speculations. Remember that you are dust, and remember, my child, how vulnerable you are to temptation. Let no pride or delusion of strength deceive you about your true condition. Your struggles are not over, and your mind easily moves into harmful areas that bring doubt, fear, and guilt.

I want you to come to a settled peace in me. It can happen. You must seek this and be willing to cooperate with me if it is to be yours.

November Tenth

For it is the God who said, "Let light shine out of darkness,"
who has shone in our hearts to give the light of the knowledge
of the glory of God in the face of Jesus Christ.
—2 Corinthians 4:6

You are blessed, my child, when your mind is stayed on me. When you allow your mind to wander in forbidden paths, thorns and pain await you. I said "allow" because you must give your mind permission to wander in paths of darkness.

My light is ever shining. It is always available to my children. I do not withhold it from those who are willing to seek it and walk in it. So choose light rather than darkness. Choose life rather than death. Choose my peace rather than torment. You are blessed when your mind is stayed on me.

November Eleventh

I know, O LORD, that your judgments are right,
and that in faithfulness you have humbled me.
—Psalm 119:75

I, the Lord, try the hearts of those I love. The furnace of affliction burns away the dross of self-love, the overgrowth of worldly cares. Though it seems hard, even cruel, it is love in action. Few understand this, and many of my children allow themselves to become confused and bewildered when the afflictions come. The heart must be tried, because it is fickle and untrustworthy. Your affections are not pure, but are mixed with personal desires that have nothing to do with my will for you. So with these "severe mercies," I trim and purge away—with your cooperation and assent. Nothing about these trials is automatic, for I do not force your will. Be aware, my child, of the quality of mercy in all your afflictions—emotional and physical. They are meant to free you of guilt, fear, and false goals.

November Twelfth

So now, O Israel, what does the Lord *your God require of you? Only
to fear the* Lord *your God, to walk in all his ways, to love him, to serve
the* Lord *your God with all your heart and with all your soul, and to
keep the commandments of the* Lord *your God and his decrees that I am
commanding you today, for your own well-being.*
—Deuteronomy 10:12–13

Morning by morning I meet with you. Morning by morning I renew my
assurance that you are loved. Steadiness of aim and purpose are required
for the race. Victory is not to the swift nor to the strong, but to those who
persevere. Any thoughts of what might lie ahead are distractions and harass-
ment of the enemy. He attacks whenever he sees a weak, unguarded place.
Be not careless or overconfident—but take care and be watchful. The battle
is still being fought, and you must do your part.

November Thirteenth

O Lord, my heart is not lifted up, my eyes are not raised too high; I do not occupy myself with things too great and too marvelous for me.
—Psalm 131:1

"The earth is the Lord's and all that is in it, the world and those who live in it" (Psalm 24:1). The rivers of Babylon and the waters of comfort are both mine. The sorrows and joys, the hopes and disappointments—all are within the compass of my care.

Do not fret yourself with things too high and too hard for you. Content yourself on the reflection of my loving care—and build up the highway of a holy life lived in my will and my presence. It is not for you to know great secrets—just to live in the greatest of all wonders—my eternal, sovereign, unchangeable love!

November Fourteenth

For in him every one of God's promises is a "Yes." For this reason it is through him that we say the "Amen," to the glory of God.
—2 Corinthians 1:20

A glimpse of glory—a glimpse of my glory has been granted to you. There are yet more glorious realities to dawn, but your sight is still obscured by sin and its consequences. Yet the glimpse of glory you have seen draws you toward the heavenly realm. Here you may have foretastes—but only foretastes of that which lies beyond. It is necessary to plod the mundane paths of your earthly life to prepare you for what I have prepared for you. Be of good cheer. They who put their trust in me will not be confounded.

November Fifteenth

As for me, I said, "O LORD, be gracious to me; heal me, for I have sinned against you."
—Psalm 41:4

Self-inflicted wounds are the hardest to heal. This is true especially of the soul. The damage to your soul by the sin of others is little compared with what you have done. This is a long-term project, my child, and it is important that you not grow weary or discouraged. It is enough that a healing is in process. The exact degree of it is not important, for what I intend is restoration and wholeness. Let patience have its perfect work, and be at peace.

November Sixteenth

It is good that one should wait quietly for the salvation of the Lord.
—Lamentations 3:26

In quietness you shall possess your soul. In stillness you shall hear my voice. Strive to enter into my rest. Learn the secret, while you yet have time, of letting go. You still cling to the old ways of anxiousness and care. Your fears are grounded in this clinging, so you are bound rather than free, troubled rather than peaceful.

Do you not know, my child, that I am the Source and Giver of the peace for which you long? Seek that peace which is mine, for in it you will be freed from the night demons of panic and terror. Claim the inheritance that is yours as my child, and do not despise my dealings. "Do not let your hearts be troubled, and do not let them be afraid" (John 14:27).

November Seventeenth

"My grace is sufficient for you, for power is made perfect in weakness."
—2 Corinthians 12:9b

Yes, I hear and am now here. I am your strength and your hope. I am the Great Physician of your soul and body, and well-acquainted with your case. Rest in the sure knowledge that grace abounds, and my power is made perfect in your weakness. You do not yet understand this, but it will become plain in my time. All is well, my child. Do not fret over the stage you are now going through.

November Eighteenth

"Come" my heart says, "seek his face!" Your face, LORD, do I seek.
Do not hide your face from me. Do not turn your servant away in
anger, you who have been my help. Do not cast me off, do not forsake me,
O God of my salvation!
—Psalm 27:8–9

There are no easy answers to the perplexities you face. There is only one answer—my sovereign grace. As light emerges from the east and lightens the whole sky, so my grace "with healing in its wings" (Malachi 4:2b) comes to you. The perplexities remain—but you do not have to be bound to them nor in them. They are smaller than they seem, and much less powerful than they appear. The light of grace will help you see them more clearly.

November Nineteenth

Trust in the LORD with all your heart, and do not
rely on your own insight.
—Proverbs 3:5

Do not seek to understand all mysteries. Thereby many have been led astray.
Let the mystery remain—a wonder and a reminder that you are not God.
I am he who reveals the secrets in their time. I disclose that which, in my
wisdom, is best. Be content to live in the incomplete—with unanswered
questions and puzzlements that you cannot decipher. In this way your soul
will grow in my likeness—and that is what I will for you.

November Twentieth

Religion that is pure and undefiled before God, the Father,
is this: to care for orphans and widows in their distress,
and to keep oneself unstained by the world.
—James 1:27

I send you out from these quiet times to live out and prove the realities you meet here. Only in the press of the day and the needs of the night can you come to know that what I tell you here is truth. Otherwise it would become an escape into an unreal world of fantasy, cut off from your real life. That is certainly not what these quiet times are meant to be. They are organically connected with the whole of your life: all your struggles, relationships, and uncertainties, your temptations and your wounds. Use them more faithfully. Recall them to mind more frequently. Refresh yourself here at the fountain of life for the heat of the day, and return hither in heart and mind in the dry season. My grace is sufficient for you.

November Twenty-first

*Then you shall take delight in the LORD, and I will make you
ride upon the heights of the earth; I will feed you with
the heritage of your ancestor Jacob. . . .*
—Isaiah 58:14a

My dear child, I delight in those who find their delight in me. I grieve for those whose delights are of this passing world. They will suffer great loss and rob themselves of many joys.

I call you to center your heart upon me. Your failures and successes are not the goal of life. The true goal is to seek and find true life in me.

I tell you again that I have loved you with an everlasting love. When fear and darkness come upon you, recall this word to your mind. Resist the accusations of the adversary that my grace is not sufficient for your needs. Oh, there is plenteous grace beyond your direst need. Am I not God? Let love cross out fear and be one of those who find their delight in me.

November Twenty-second

We destroy arguments and every proud obstacle raised up against the knowledge of God, and we take every thought captive to obey Christ.
—2 Corinthians 10:4c–5

As wandering sheep inevitably stray into dangerous places, the wandering mind strays into darkness. The path of light is a safe path for you, my child, but your own path is filled with briars and thorns. Has it not been so? The effort to stay in the lighted way is to fight the entrance of tempting thoughts. Recognizing the enemy's attempt to gain entrance into your thoughts and will is an important part of the battle. Your record here is not good. Too often you grieve my Spirit by playing the fool before his advances. Wake up to the reality that life is a battleground, and will be to the end.

November Twenty-third

I will rejoice in Jerusalem, and delight in my people. . . .
—Isaiah 65:19a

I, the Lord God, Maker of heaven and earth, delight to hold fellowship with my lowly creatures. My love created them and gave them life and breath. My Spirit quickened them into new life, to enable them to seek me and find me in the appointed time. Do not marvel that such is the case, for it is the nature of love to seek the good and happiness of others. My delight can only be increased as my children find true joy and delight. My divine happiness, my joy, is increased by theirs. The joy that was set before me on the cross was the sure faith-knowledge that my death would bring joy and delight to my children.

I do not seek cowardly servants, but joyful children. I do not find pleasure in fear-inspired service, though I accept it as a stage toward maturity. When the fullness of love comes, our relation can be based on a mutual desire to bring joy to the other. Learning to see my design in purging out false dreams and aims is a step—a necessary step in the path to maturity. The tapestry of my plan begins to "make sense" as you view your life in this light.

November Twenty-fourth

O taste and see that the LORD is good; happy are
those who take refuge in him.
—Psalm 34:8

Never fear to speak the word I give you. Fear will quench the free-flowing of
my Spirit. Boldness is needed, because it always exposes you to humiliation.

It is necessary for you to venture forth with the words I give you, not
knowing where they will lead or what will come next. As you can see, they
do go somewhere and bring a blessing with them.

I am pleased when you calmly wait in obedience, not fretting or strain-
ing. Let your heart rest in me, and feed your soul on the manna of my love.

November Twenty-fifth

Blessed be the LORD, *the God of Israel, from everlasting to everlasting.*
And let all the people say, "Amen." Praise the LORD!
—Psalm 106:48

My child, your thankfulness gladdens my heart and strengthens yours. It truly is a *good* thing to be thankful, because gratitude aligns your soul with my Spirit and opens you to the healing streams of my mercy. My heart is always gladdened when any child of mine becomes open to my mercy. Gratitude opens the "channels of reception," which are necessary for you to receive the blessings I would willingly pour out on you. Gratitude is an antidote to false pride and its distortions of the soul. It is an antidote to fear, because the soul recognizes the benevolence and good will which lay behind the gift. Gratitude opens the channels of fellowship and charity, because it kills false competition and jealousy.

I have called you many times to praise and give thanks. My Word exhorts my people to give thanks. These are some of the inner reasons why praise is essential for your life with me. Praise opens clogged channels, and the soul can grow stronger in the purer sunlight of my love and goodness when it turns away from itself and exercises this holy privilege.

Yes, my child, your thankfulness gladdens my heart and strengthens yours.

November Twenty-sixth

See, the LORD'S hand is not too short to save, nor his ear too dull to hear.
Rather, your iniquities have been barriers between you and your God,
and your sins have hidden his face from you so that he does not hear.
—Isaiah 59:1–2

You come to me laden with cares. I come to you laden with peace. When you turn your cares into prayer, my peace prevails. No anxiety has room here between us, my child. Do not worry about yourself or others—for then you bring only your unbelief. My arm is not shortened that it cannot reach those for whom you care. My promises are not so weak that circumstances can blot them out. Cast your cares on me. Turn them into faith-filled prayer. Rejoice in what I have already done and let your face be lightened. No room for anxiety here, my child—only faith, hope, thanksgiving, and praise. I come to you laden with peace. Accept it and abide in it.

November Twenty-seventh

When he has brought out all his own, he goes ahead of them, and the
sheep follow him because they know his voice.
—John 10:4

My voice is a mighty voice. My voice is a still, small voice. I speak in tones designed to carry out my will. Your ear is still too much attuned to your own voice and the voice of the world. Silence is essential to tuning in to my words to you. Do not think time is wasted in waiting. Do not grow impatient or disheartened that it takes you so long. Remember how long you have lived without this necessary preparation—and how sporadic and scattered were the times you "heard" my voice. I have had to speak in the loud tones of circumstances—some of them drastic—to guide you in my chosen way. But I would prefer to speak in the still, small voice, and see you willingly hear and obey. So I bid you, my child, do not give up on your waiting and listening—and learn to be still and know my voice.

November Twenty-eighth

. . . and he upbraided them for their lack of faith and stubbornness. . . .
—Mark 16:14b

Yes, you are fearful to open the door of your heart to my voice. You are afraid of what I will say about your sins. And so this delay in our communion, while you "dance about," insisting that you want to hear my word to you. You are still divided, and pride still rules where humility should reign. O proud and foolish one! How long will you linger in the shades of separation when we might be walking together in the path of light? I am grieved at your slowness of heart. I appeal to you by my many mercies—give up this pride and get on with it!

November Twenty-ninth

I am the God of mercy. Your life, my child, is a manifestation of it. You have not chosen me, but I have chosen you, and set my mercy upon you. In a vessel such as you are—weak, unstable, hidden, and high-minded—only my mercy can bring forth any lasting good. The unlovable elements in your nature work against that mercy—war against it—striving for ascendancy and recognition. They are *always* self-defeating. They produce their own punishment. But my mercies fail not. And your life is meant to show the fruit that grows from both. Let mercy prevail!

November Thirtieth

He leads the humble in what is right, and teaches the humble his way.
—Psalm 25:9

This is my word today: carry out the gentle nudges and quiet thoughts that come to you. Do not allow your disbelief to rob you of my intended blessing. Nothing else can hinder it. Believe, act, and see.

DECEMBER

Jesus, thou divine
      Companion, By thy lowly
      human birth
Thou hast come to join the
      workers, Burden-bearers of
      the earth.
Thou, the carpenter of Nazareth,
      Toiling for thy daily food,
By thy patience and thy
      courage, thou hast taught us
      toil is good.
Where the many toil together,
      There art thou among thine own;
Where the tired workman
      sleepeth,
      There art thou with him alone;
Thou, the peace that passeth
      knowledge,
      Dwellest in the daily strife;
Thou, the Bread of heaven, art
      broken in the sacrament of life.
Every task, however simple,
      Sets the soul that does it free;
Every deed of love and kindness
      Done to man is done to thee.
Jesus, thou divine Companion,
      Help us all to work our best;
Bless us in our daily labor,
      Lead us to our Sabbath rest.

—Henry van Dyke, 1852–1933

December First

*. . . then within me there is something like a burning fire shut up
in my bones; I am weary with holding it in, and I cannot.*
—Jeremiah 20:9b

My word is a fire—a purging, purifying fire—burning the dross and refuse of
the years past. My word destroys as well as it builds. It must destroy strongholds
of darkness and rebellion. You do not even know where or what some of those
strongholds are in your soul. They must be assaulted and destroyed that you
might be whole in me. My word is not always in words. My word is my will
going forth from me to accomplish my purpose. You may tremble or weep
before it without consciously knowing why or what is being done. Do not
worry. Submit yourself "so far as it depends on you" (Romans 12:18a) to my
sovereign purpose. Keep silent before my mysterious ways, for all will be light
in the end. Faith requires this, to trust where you are mystified, to hold on to
what I have said when the outward conditions seem to contradict it. This is the
way and walk of faith.

December Second

You show me the path of life. In your presence there is fullness of joy;
in your right hand are pleasures forevermore.
—Psalm 16:11

Draw near to me, and I will draw near to you. I am ever near, but you are usually unmindful of it. It takes a conscious choice on your part to enter into a realization that I am here.

My aim and purpose for you, my child, is for you to dwell in my presence. In my presence there is fullness of joy. In my presence is peace that passes understanding. But in my presence there is no room for self-absorption and self-promotion. These things must die and be purged away. They are deadly and death-giving. They must die so that *life*, true life, my life, can be yours.

Bless the means by which I further my plan for you. Keep before your eyes what I have told you. In my presence there is fullness of joy.

December Third

Cast all your anxiety on him, because he cares for you.
—I Peter 5:7

Cast your anxiety on me, and I will sustain you. I am he who bears the burden of the weak. You have not yet learned the secret of my burden-bearing, and you inflict pain on yourself and others in your reaction to situations you feel are unjust or unfair. You still demand that others think of you the way you think of yourself, and in your determination not to come under their "false accusations," you strike or lash back. My dear child, you do not have to do this! You are a sin-bearer, and I am ready to enter the situation with healing if you will cast your burden upon me. Your way has never worked—so why not try mine?

December Fourth

. . . we are his people, and the sheep of his pasture.
—Psalm 100:3b

I know my sheep and call them by name. This is a mystery beyond your comprehension, for you rightly see how impossible it is for the human mind. But I am the God of the impossible—by which I mean that my power and ability far exceed any thought you might have of me—however grand and majestic it might be. In my choice to become man and dwell among you, I did not diminish my infinity. Your life has been too confined by your mental boundaries. You have severely limited your participation in my divine greatness by these boundaries. But hear this word again and meditate on it. It contains a key to unlock resources you have not dreamed of or yet experienced. I *know* my sheep and call them by name. My dear child, that little word can make all the difference—if you learn to believe it.

December Fifth

. . . these follow the Lamb wherever he goes. . . .
—Revelation 14:4b

As the eagle flies upward, above the noise and strife of this busy world, so should your soul fly upward to commune with me. Most of your life has been lived in the lowlands—your thoughts and imaginations—even your dreams—have lodged there. Take this invitation seriously, my child, while there is yet time. Do not worry about what others are doing or thinking—for that is but a weight and hindrance to you. Seek my face. Seek to know me in myself—not hearsay or opinion—but a living knowledge that I will impart, if you will "follow the Lamb wherever he goes." Be bold in your need and do not fear to draw near.

December Sixth

"Everyone who belongs to the truth listens to my voice."
—John 18:37c

My child, I often speak to you in quiet tones, but my voice is drowned by
your busy thoughts. You must learn, as you have begun to learn, to *listen*.
My Spirit is life and brings life. Your spirit has no life of itself. I shall not
leave you until I have accomplished that which I have begun in you. Be
prepared to change. Do not be afraid. Already the hour is late, but there is
ample time. Be sensitive to the leading that comes, checking your old habits
and patterns of thought, action, and reaction. Hunger and thirst for more
of me, of my life and my way. Even now the old is passing away, and will
pass—if you will let it go. You do not have to understand—only trust—and
see my glory revealed. O my child, do you not see the wonder of my love?

December Seventh

Let me hear of your steadfast love in the morning, for in you I put my trust. Teach me the way I should go, for to you I lift up my soul.
—Psalm 143:8

I have given my Spirit to abide in you and to guide you into all truth. My truth is too large for your limited mind, and sometimes you meet with what seems to be contradictions. These confuse you and confound your arrogant self-righteousness. You remember how you struggled with the accounts of the Resurrection many years ago—and suffered because you could not make them match up. Even then, I was dealing with one of your most serious sins—your demand to understand everything in black and white. This was meant to humble you and to quiet your incessant yearning to understand all mysteries.

Your life now is full of mysteries you cannot explain. I have surrounded you with many things for which your heart longed from childhood. Remember that as you enjoy the unfolding of the beauty of my world. I saw and felt the yearning you knew, and in my love and grace, I have satisfied the desire of your spirit. Receive these tokens of my goodness and let them bring new depths of gratitude to your heart. Do you see how these gifts are also dimensions of my truth! There are wonders yet to be unfolded. Trust and follow your guide.

December Eighth

". . . for the devil has come down to you with great wrath, because he knows that his time is short!"
—Revelation 12:12b

Come with me, my child, into the future I have prepared for you. The years and the ages are mine, and I am a safe guide and companion.

The past is covered by my redeeming sacrifice. It lives in your memory to be a perpetual reminder of your sinful nature and of my grace. You have seen how I have moved to redeem that which was beyond your control, and what I have done, I am still able to do.

This world, in all its brokenness and darkness, is still the world for which I laid down my life. The enemy is still not convinced that my victory is complete, so with great wrath he snatches whomever he can. Prayer is a mighty weapon against his power. Do not forget this. Prayer *does* make a difference, because I have made a place for it in my divine plan. So keep praying as my Spirit directs and leads—and do not forget my little ones. O, do not forget my little ones!

December Ninth

So deeply do we care for you that we are determined to share with
you not only the gospel of God but also our own selves,
because you have become very dear to us.
—1 Thessalonians 2:8

My child, do not grieve over the things that are lost to you. Strengthen the things that remain. I have taken nothing from you that is of eternal value. I remove in order to fulfill. I take away that I might give. My way is always to supply what you need in abundance, even when that abundance feels like deprivation.

My generosity to you is commensurate with my mercy. It is never-failing and always in right proportion. So there is no cause for worry or anxiety, but much cause for gratitude and rejoicing.

I note your sense of loss in relationships—and say again to you: do not grieve over those who are lost to you. They are not lost to me or to my divine mercy. Rest in the assurance that I am faithful and know what is best. That for you can be a place of settled rest.

December Tenth

Then Moses said, "I must turn aside and look at this
great sight, and see why the bush is not burned up."
—Exodus 3:3

It is my delight to see my children seeking my face. Seek and you shall find. Knock and it shall be opened to you. I am found by those who seek, ask, look—and I *never* turn away any sincere soul.

Wonders are common with the souls that truly seek my face. For this reason, you are likely to become a little peculiar in the eyes of others—even those close to you. Turning aside to the burning bush, listening for my voice, obeying my commands—these all set you apart from what is considered ordinary and normal. But you must not allow this privilege to make you special in your own eyes. Rather let it make you more aware of how utterly dependent you are for daily strength and for wisdom to decide between good and evil.

Bring your hurts and your sins here, my child. The throne of grace is open to you—and to all who seek my face. Give up defending yourself—learn from me—and seek my help in overcoming this fault.

December Eleventh

Beloved, we are God's children now; what we will be has not yet been revealed. What we do know is this: when he is revealed, we will be like him, for we will see him as he is.
—1 John 3:2

Blessed indeed are you, my child, to be called into the fellowship of the redeemed. Happy, three times happy, are those who forsake their ways and follow me. My plan of redemption encompasses the beginning, the middle, and the end. Along the way the discarded ways are left behind. The dreams and ambitions fade, shrivel, and die. The sins are revealed, and repented, and forgiven. The rebellions are put down and the wars cease. This must all take place before the full happiness to which I have called you can be experienced.

Yes, I have called you to happiness—by which I mean the cup of joy, the internal harmony and peace, and the full realization of my love, which as yet you but dimly see. On such a case as yours I set my love and prove again that I am conqueror over the fall. The price is high, but I chose to pay it, and choose to carry it to final victory in souls like yours.

December Twelfth

"But about that day and hour no one knows, neither the angels of heaven, nor the Son, but only the Father. . . . Therefore you also must be ready, for the Son of Man is coming at an unexpected hour."
—Matthew 24:36, 44

The mystery of my coming will always remain. It is not yours to understand but to receive. It is hidden for my purpose and in my purpose. Expect that I will come to you, my child, in my own time and way—bringing blessing and the gift of myself. Do not think, wrongly, that it is a light gift. Keep watching and expecting—till I come.

December Thirteenth

". . . I go to prepare a place for you. . . . I will come again and will take you to myself, so that where I am, you may be also."
—John 14:2b–3b

Don't give up! Don't give in! The small growth in your perception of my love for you can encourage you to persevere in the path I am placing before you. Remember, my child, that I take the long view in our walk together. What you cannot see or imagine is crystal-clear to me, and so I bear with you in your struggles. Your failures are less disturbing to me than to you. So don't give up! Don't give in! The struggles are worth more than gold, because they move you along the path. You will not be disappointed.

December Fourteenth

. . . I have set my face like flint, and I know that
I shall not be put to shame. . . .
—Isaiah 50:7b

My word to you today is: stay. Stay on the course I have laid out for you. Keep your mind and thoughts on me. Stay within the bounds of my will, and you will know my peace. Stay by me in prayer and thanksgiving. Stay with my word that is able to keep you from being led astray in strange paths. Stop the hand of the wicked one with prayer. Remain on the course. Finish your race with joy. I will not leave you alone. I *will not* leave you alone. Banish such thoughts and fears, knowing where they come from.

December Fifteenth

. . . since all have sinned and fall short of the glory of God;
they are now justified by his grace as a gift, through the
redemption that is in Christ Jesus. . . .
—Romans 3:23–24

My dear child, mourn your sins but rejoice in my saving love. Repent of all that is in you that resists and rebels against my will, but rejoice that my grace is all-sufficient—even for you. Your proud and arrogant nature pollutes much of your relationship with others and with me. It separates and isolates you from true communion and true fellowship. Add to that your memories of past sins and hurts, and you are rendered incapable of doing laudable service—except for my overruling grace. The more you see and recognize this, the freer you will become to move into a grace-filled life. You are still choosing, too often, the old paths. They are death. Choose life. To live you must die to the old and embrace the giving up of its temporary satisfactions—however costly the giving up may appear. Let them win! Give up your demand to be accepted and recognized. Hide yourself internally in my side. Do it in love, not in self-pity or vindictiveness. Allow me to become your all.

December Sixteenth

*Then I looked, and I heard the voice of many angels surrounding the
throne and the living creatures and the elders; they numbered myriads of
myriads, and thousands of thousands, singing with full voice, "Worthy is
the Lamb that was slaughtered to receive power and wealth and wisdom
and might and honor and glory and blessing!"*
—Revelation 5:11–12

More and more as you turn to me, your time and thoughts should be spent
in praise and thanksgiving. Heaven, after all, is a place of praise. There,
with full vision, and understanding clarified, there is neither sorrow nor
crying nor vain regrets—but praise filling every heart. As you give yourself to
praise here, you enter the heavenly realm. Your praise, inadequate as it is, unites
with that of the heavenly family—and is magnified in the process. "Let the
humble hear and be glad" (Psalm 33:2b).

Take this thought, my child, and dwell on it. Your negative and fearful
thought-life must be attacked on many levels—and none is more important
than this one.

December Seventeenth

"Lord, if another member of the church sins against me, how often should I forgive? As many as seven times?" Jesus said to him, "Not seven times, but I tell you, seventy—seven times."
—Matthew 18:21b–22

My yoke is easy and my burden is light. I impose no harsh duties on my children. The hardest lesson for you to learn is my gentleness. Your own harsh nature reflects the desire to see your enemy suffer. Such satisfaction is short-lived, and brings its own bitterness with it. You have the opportunity in your present life situation to bear my easy yoke and learn of me. Learn to forgive. Learn how light a burden I ask you to bear. Lack of forgiveness is a heavy one—and unnecessary.

December Eighteenth

Therefore, as the Holy Spirit says, "Today, if you hear his voice,
do not harden your hearts . . ."
—Hebrews 3:7–8a

My word to you is this: today if you hear my word, do not harden your heart. The encrustation of self-defense is like corrosion on metal. It forms a protective and insulating barrier against the truth. In the meantime its corrosive effect is also at work, tearing down even the good that has already been done. This is why I said in Scripture, "the last state of that person is worse than the first" (Matthew 12:45b). The deadness, apathy, the inability to be inwardly moved—these are indicators that damage has already been done.

There is no sin that does a more deadly work to the soul than hardening the heart. So I say again, "Today if you hear [my] word, do not harden your hearts." "Let anyone with ears to hear, listen" (Mark 4:9).

December Nineteenth

I waited patiently for the LORD; he inclined to me and heard my cry.
—Psalm 40:1

You wait to hear my word. Remember, my child, how long I have waited for you. Remember my patient perseverance as your mind was led in strange and vain paths. Yes, I waited for your return, knowing that a seed of faith had been planted in you. You must also be patient and persevering in awaiting my visitation. Do not think that this exercise is in vain, for I never arrive too late. Let my word be an encouragement to you in the days ahead, when delay seems long. Persevere.

December Twentieth

"Come to me, all you who are weary and are carrying heavy burdens, and I will give you rest. Take my yoke upon you, and learn from me; for I am gentle and humble in heart, and you will find rest for your souls. For my yoke is easy, and my burden is light."
—Matthew 11:28–30

I have heard your prayer, my child. I never turn a deaf ear to my children. I am not such a one as you, nor as you perceive me to be. You do not yet know or fathom the depth of my love. Your proud nature, though wounded by many blows, by my permission, still distorts your vision of me. I am meek and lowly in heart, and here—in my merciful presence—you shall find rest unto your soul. Where is boasting here? Where is glory? Where is calculation of merits and good works? Where is condemnation? Not here—not any of these things. None are relevant when you enter this place of rest. I am here—the meek and lowly one. I am here—he who forgives your iniquities and heals your diseases. I am here—your health and salvation. And when you turn—truly turn to me—do you not realize that my love is satisfied, and the travail of my soul is satisfied in that turning? For this I suffered. For this I died—that you might turn to me and know how much you are loved. Don't be afraid of my love. Don't hesitate to turn to me.

December Twenty-first

"After this I will return, and I will rebuild the dwelling of David,
which has fallen; from its ruins I will rebuild it, and I will set it up, so
that all other peoples may seek the Lord. . . ."
Acts 15:16–17a

Vain regrets are vanity. They are empty clouds bearing no water and no life. Many decisions in the past were wrong and carried with them seeds of suffering. Some of that suffering is in seeking consequences undreamed of—and bitter. Vain regret cannot change the past. The seeds of suffering germinate and grow, bringing their inevitable fruit. Without me this would be a tragic tale—and life would, indeed, be sad.

But I am the Lord who builds out of ruins. Sometimes ruins are the only material I can use, and all that was promising and beautiful must be allowed to crumble and fall before the real work of lasting beauty can rise. Look well at the fruit of folly, the pain of plans, and dreams gone awry. Then look to me, at what I am doing—yes, I the Lord am doing a new thing. In every situation where the seed of suffering is flowering and bearing fruit, I am at work on the ruins. Keep looking, and your sorrow will turn to joy in the morning.

December Twenty-second

. . . this grace was given to me to bring to the Gentiles the news of the boundless riches of Christ, and to make everyone see what is the plan of the mystery hidden for ages in God who created all things; so that through the church the wisdom of God in its rich variety might now be made known to the rulers and authorities in the heavenly places. This was in accordance with the eternal purpose that he has carried out in Christ Jesus our Lord. . . .
—Ephesians 3:8b–11

As you draw near to the commemoration of my birth, I want you to see why there is so little information given about its details. The human mind craves particulars. But my coming among you is a mystery—and must remain wrapped in mystery if it is to convey its deepest truth. So do not be misled into thinking that more facts mean more truth. Let the mystery remain—and wonder.

December Twenty-third

*When you search for me, you will find me; if you seek
for me with all your heart. . . .*
—Jeremiah 29:13

You are coming to the feast of my humiliation. It is not that I was humbled by men, but that I chose this path of my own sovereign will. No shame clung to the circumstances, because it was my loving, saving purpose behind it. You can rid yourself of false shame in your humiliations if you will learn from me. At the present time, you still carry this unnecessary burden and it hampers your witness to my mercy in your life. Despise the shame, my child—and accept my gracious dealings—including your humiliations.

December Twenty-fourth

Fight the good fight of the faith; take hold of the eternal life,
to which you were called. . .
—I Timothy 6:12a

This is my word to you today, my child. Keep diligently what I have committed to you. The time is short. The days are evil. Look for the manifestation of my glory. Put away childish ways—and let your faith in me grow more childlike. Deny your desire for vindication and acceptance. Put down your appetite for place and power. Take a seat among the lowly—and there you will find sweet companionship with me.

Remember, my child, that when I came to earth, it was in a stable that my mother gave me birth. Honor and love her—for her suffering and faithful patience. Let her be an example of the soul that finds favor with God. I still dwell among the lowly in heart. There you can always count on finding me.

December Twenty-fifth

. . . he has made known to us the mystery of his will. . . .
—Ephesians 1:9a

Quiet, my child! Be quiet before the mystery. Silence suits you as you think with awe on what I have done. My presence is an oasis of peace in this angry, troubled world. You have yet to learn to be silenced before my mystery. Eternity does not enter the thoughts of the angry soul. Let my haven of peace, the lowly stable, be a refuge from your anger and ambitions. Quiet, my child, and think on the mystery of the ages—and be at peace.

December Twenty-sixth

*"It is the spirit that gives life; the flesh is useless. The words
that I have spoken to you are spirit and life."*
—John 6:63

Quiet your soul before me, and I will speak. Your usual chatter drowns out
the still, small voice of my Spirit. Do not be afraid of inner quiet. I am your
protector and your defender. Be still and know. Be still and hear. Be still and
experience the wonders of my love and grace. I wait to be gracious—yes, I,
the Lord, wait for my children to still their own voices that they may hear
mine. You, my child, still have a long way to go to learn to do this readily
and easily. Your chatter is really mental clutter. Let me help you become more
uncluttered—and thus more at peace with yourself and with me. My peace
I give to you—as you are prepared to accept it.

December Twenty-seventh

*I formed you, you are my servant; O Israel, you will not be
forgotten by me. . . . return to me, for I have redeemed you.*
—Isaiah 44:21b–22

In the womb of the morning new life is begotten. My Spirit quickens and
brings life anew. Doubt not that it is so, but throw off the old and put on
that newness I bring.

December Twenty-eighth

For the LORD is good; his steadfast love endures forever,
and his faithfulness to all generations.
—Psalm 100:5

The generations rise and pass away before me. You see and experience sadness as your own generation draws nearer to the grave. Soon, very soon, you will all be forgotten by the living. Only a few from each generation are remembered. But I do not forget. These brief years on earth—with their sorrows, hopes, and joys—are not the whole of my gift of life.

I am the God of the living—and my gift of life goes on for those who come to me for life. My care and my love do not end with the grave—so do not look with sad eyes at the brevity of your life here. Open them to the beauty of holiness and grace. Let these final years be both a finishing and a beginning—for my gift of life is an unending one.

December Twenty-ninth

The LORD is good to all, and his compassion
is over all that he has made.
—Psalm 145:9

In my mercy there is provision for your every need. My ways seem strange to you, and sometimes you rebel against them. But in so doing, you are rebelling against my mercy.

A frightened bird can do itself much harm in trying to escape the loving attention of a well-intentioned person. Even so, you can bring harm to yourself in refusing my mercy when you don't recognize it.

This world calls such acceptance unreality "Pollyannaish." But I call it a pearl of great price, a treasure hid in the field of your life—a trust like Mary's that allowed my purpose to proceed without hindrance or delay. Remember, my child, my *tender* mercies are over all my works. In my mercy there is provision for your every need.

December Thirtieth

For with you is the fountain of life; in your light we see light.
—Psalm 36:9

Look to the sunrise! Look to the day-dawn. Turn from the darkness; do not dwell on the shadows of the night. My glory is in the dawn. My way is open. There is light on your path—the light of truth and the sure word of my promise. O my child, rejoice in the light. Cast away dark thoughts and fear-laden burdens, and be a light-follower. "Whoever follows me will never walk in darkness, but will have the light of life" (John 8:12b). Look to the sunrise!

December Thirty-first

They said to him, "Rabbi" (which translated means Teacher), "where are you staying?" He said to them, "Come and see."
—John 1:38b–39a

The way before you is a good way. You do not need to see the distant views, but keep your eye on the present choices. I have not called you to be a purposeless wasteland, but to be a fruitful field, to bear fruit for my kingdom. You do not need to know where or how this will come about. Your pride must not be fed in the process. But I will tell you this—you do not need to fear being left adrift or cast aside. Those are thoughts of self, and they have no place in our relationship. So be about my business. Put aside the murmurings of your old nature, your yearnings for gratification that you sought in "place" and "respect." Let go of these things for my sake, and each time you feel a wound, bring it to me for forgiveness. Pride dies hard, so don't be surprised that it is still struggling for life in you.

Deo gratias.

Reflections

Reflections

Reflections

Reflections

Reflections

Reflections

About Paraclete Press

Who We Are

Paraclete Press is a publisher of books, recordings, and DVDs on Christian spirituality. Our publishing represents a full expression of Christian belief and practice—from Catholic to Evangelical, from Protestant to Orthodox.

We are the publishing arm of the Community of Jesus, an ecumenical monastic community in the Benedictine tradition. As such, we are uniquely positioned in the marketplace without connection to a large corporation and with informal relationships to many branches and denominations of faith.

What We Are Doing

PARACLETE PRESS BOOKS | Paraclete publishes books that show the richness and depth of what it means to be Christian. Although Benedictine spirituality is at the heart of all that we do, we publish books that reflect the Christian experience across many cultures, time periods, and houses of worship. We publish books that nourish the vibrant life of the church and its people.

We have several different series, including the best-selling Paraclete Essentials and Paraclete Giants series of classic texts in contemporary English; Voices from the Monastery—men and women monastics writing about living a spiritual life today; award-winning poetry; best-selling gift books for children on the occasions of baptism and first communion; and the Active Prayer Series that brings creativity and liveliness to any life of prayer.

MOUNT TABOR BOOKS | Paraclete's newest series, Mount Tabor Books, focuses on the arts and literature as well as liturgical worship and spirituality, and was created in conjunction with the Mount Tabor Ecumenical Centre for Art and Spirituality in Barga, Italy.

PARACLETE RECORDINGS | From Gregorian chant to contemporary American choral works, our recordings celebrate the best of sacred choral music composed through the centuries that create a space for heaven and earth to intersect. Paraclete Recordings is the record label representing the internationally acclaimed choir Gloriæ Dei Cantores, praised for their "rapt and fathomless spiritual intensity" by American Record Guide; the Gloriæ Dei Cantores Schola, specializing in the study and performance of Gregorian chant; and the other instrumental artists of the Gloriæ Dei Artes Foundation.

Paraclete Press is also privileged to be the exclusive North American distributor of the recordings of the Monastic Choir of St. Peter's Abbey in Solesmes, France, long considered to be a leading authority on Gregorian chant.

PARACLETE VIDEO | Our DVDs offer spiritual help, healing, and biblical guidance for a broad range of life issues including grief and loss, marriage, forgiveness, facing death, bullying, addictions, Alzheimer's, and spiritual formation.

Learn more about us at our website:
www.paracletepress.com or phone us
toll-free at 1.800.451.5006

SCAN TO READ MORE

Generous Faith
Stories to Inspire Abundant Living
SISTER BRIDGET HAASE, osu

978-1-55725-615-7 • $16.99 Paperback

This simple and joy-filled book opens our hearts to what is in the air we breathe, under our feet and in this very moment: the abundant life, a gift from God. As Sr. Bridget says with her infectious enthusiasm, all we need to do is cultivate this awareness through living in the moment, trusting in Divine care and experiencing God's presence. This book is guaranteed to help you to re-examine your own faith journey and give you a fresh perspective.

Holy Spirit, I Pray
JACK LEVISON

978-1-61261-683-4 • $13.99 Leatherette

Meet the Holy Spirt as you never have before, and discover the hidden reality of the Spirit tucked away in everyday life. In this book, each raw, honest prayer of uncanny candor and surprising beauty is accompanied by the Scripture texts that inspired it. "Jack Levison studies, meditates, prays, and writes of the place of the Holy Spirit in our lives with more skill and understanding than anyone I know."
—Eugene Peterson, author/translator of *The Message*

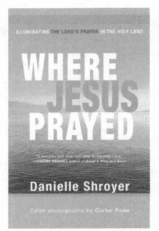

Where Jesus Prayed
DANIELLE SHROYER

978-1-61261-661-2 • $16.99 Paperback

"Danielle's beautiful and wise 'love letter to the Holy Land' brought me right back to the smells, sounds, and textures of that extraordinary place, and it drew me into a deeper connection with the Lord's Prayer along the way. This book is an invitation to walk with Jesus in a richer way, and I've learned from every step along that journey."
—Shauna Niequist, author of *Bread & Wine* and *Savor*

Available through your local bookseller or through Paraclete Press:
www.paracletepress.com; 1-800-451-5006